OUT OF THE
DARKNESS

MATT PIPER
WITH JOE BREWIN

OUT OF THE
DARKNESS
MY STORY IN FOOTBALL

FROM
TOP TO
ROCK
BOTTOM

First published by Pitch Publishing, 2020

Pitch Publishing
A2 Yeoman Gate
Yeoman Way
Worthing
Sussex
BN13 3QZ
www.pitchpublishing.co.uk
info@pitchpublishing.co.uk

A CIP catalogue record is available for this book
from the British Library.

ISBN 978 1 78531 652 4

Typesetting and origination by Pitch Publishing

Printed and bound in India by Replika Press Pvt. Ltd.

Contents

For Leanne, Brandan, Finlay, Kairo and Sienna – I love you with every piece of my heart. Everything I do is for you.

Foreword

By Brian Deane

WHEN YOU go into a new football club as a senior professional, you immediately scout around and survey your new environment. I joined Leicester City from Middlesbrough in November 2001, when the club was struggling in the Premiership* relegation zone. Not much was going right for them back then.

But it wasn't all bad. I remember speaking to someone who told me, 'We've got a lad here who is going to be something special. He's quick, his feet are ridiculous, and technically he's going to go all the way.'

I hadn't heard of Matt Piper before that conversation – he'd only made his senior debut the previous month – and in fact, he wasn't even at the club when I arrived. He was on loan at Mansfield for a couple of months and returned to Leicester that January, having done very well in his time away from Filbert Street.

Then I quickly started to see what the fuss was all about.

What was really nice was how humble a young lad Matt was – he wasn't cocky or anything like that. The other players of his peer group were a lot chattier than he was, but Matt was just generally a lovely kid. It made me think, 'I want to help and look out for him if I can.'

At first, I told him to remember that he was in the first-team group because he was good enough. Sometimes, young lads come up to train with the pros but don't believe they should be there; that they're just making up the numbers. In fairness, sometimes they are. But because Matt was a quiet guy, it was important to stress that he was there for a reason. It was his opportunity to grow.

And he did. I remember the skinny legs and that people already knew he'd had some issues with his knees by then, but he seemed to glide whenever he had the ball. I never saw the pace that everybody talked about, but I remember left-back Jordan Stewart – who was rapid himself – telling me that Matt was on another level to him. He had a different gear. I thought, 'Wow – he's got all of that *and* he's quick?'

In early-February 2002, we played Chelsea at Filbert Street. Matt put Marcel Desailly in a world of trouble, and I knew then that he had something to get excited about. He had come into that environment at 20 and proved very quickly that he could do it against a guy who'd won the World Cup, European Championship and Champions League. When I got a bit older, I started to take more of an interest in sports psychology – but I didn't need any special expertise to see that Marcel realised he'd had a very hard time with Pipes that afternoon. Generally, you learn to give off certain signals as an older pro to suggest you're having no problems, but Marcel couldn't even manage that in this particular game.

Sadly for Matt, his time at the club came to an end sooner than he would have liked it to. Leicester were relegated in 2002, and there were good reasons why the club needed to sell him that summer; their financial problems at the time were well documented. He didn't want to leave, but asked a few of the older pros for some advice about what to do – so I gave it to him straight. 'The club want to sell you, Matty – you've got to go. If you stay, you might not be welcome. You'd be going to a Premiership club, and that's the best stage for you right now.' He was better suited to the top flight at that time, anyway.

I tried to be like a bigger brother to Matt and a few of the other lads at Leicester who were coming into the game. I was at the end of my career and facing a time when there wouldn't be football in my life for much longer. I remembered being a young lad myself, thinking that I was going to live to be 100 years old and do everything I'd ever wanted to do, but you start to see your own mortality when you get a bit older. All I was trying to do was say, 'Look guys, nothing is going to last forever. You have a massive opportunity now, so make the most of it; be the best you can be. That way, you'll learn about what you are going to become. But if you don't take it seriously, then you have a problem.'

As it turned out, it wouldn't be the last time our careers crossed paths. When I arrived at Sunderland for a brief spell in 2005, it was obvious that Matt had suffered some problems there. We didn't really talk much about them at the time, but the move hadn't gone the way he'd wanted it to. He felt like he'd let people down – including himself. But sometimes, it just doesn't work out for you. Transfers create challenges in themselves: he'd gone up there with a big pay rise in an environment that was nowhere near as familiar to him as Leicester; far away from familiar faces and what he knew. I didn't stay at the Stadium of Light for long before heading to Australia, but we kept in touch afterwards when his life began to take a darker turn.

I nearly fell out with Matt once. I had a friend who knew that he meant a lot to me and introduced herself to him once as a pal of mine. He wasn't particularly nice to her – apparently, worse for wear and steaming in a club – and it was reported back to me. I got on the phone to him and told him he was out of order. 'If that's how you're going to be, then fine – you and I are done.' I was willing to fall out with him at that point. It hurt me. I'd always spoken glowingly of him, but that made me re-evaluate. I wasn't willing to say to him, 'What's going on?' – instead, it was 'stop being a dickhead'.

People who knew Matt during his football career and know him today wouldn't recognise that in him. The way he has turned his life around since then has been nothing short of amazing, and he has actually inspired me in a lot of ways along the way. He started coaching, and I looked at some of the things he was talking about doing – his own YouTube channel, for example – in awe.

It was all so positive. Matt had looked up to me for a lot of his career, but there were times when I needed some guidance, too. I took some inspiration from what he was doing, and whether he knows it or not, it helped me through some of my own more difficult times. You're never too old to learn.

By seeing what he was doing and how he'd transformed his life, it inspired me. I know at one point he was in a dark place with a young family, wondering what might happen next. But eventually, he found the resilience he needed to get him through life and into a place where he's now making a real positive difference to others.

I'm so proud of him.

The Premier League was called the Premiership from 1993-2007.

PROLOGUE

The cat with no more lives

19 January 2006

I am no longer a professional footballer. It's over – all of it. The dreams I had when I was a kid? Gone. I am no longer Matt Piper the Premiership player at Sunderland.

And do you know what my first thought is?

Thank fuck for that.

When I look back on that day, I remember the feeling was pure relief. My knees had been a mess since I was 16 years old – by the end, I'd lost count of the operations, injections, physio sessions and consultations; the constant rehab that seemed never-ending. Twenty years of development for 55 professional games over five years. Sunderland owed me over £1.1 million to the end of my contract, but I couldn't care less. I took a quarter of that and ran.

A few months before the end, there had been an incident. During my rehabilitation, I would go into Sunderland's

14

training ground early and swim 50 lengths before I went in to see the physio each day – I was dedicated to getting back fit every single time, no matter what. But that day, I had a panic attack in the pool; the only one I'd ever had as a footballer … if not the last I was to have in my life. If only it had been the last.

At the time, I didn't want to tell anyone because I was worried that the club would get rid of me. All of that stress building up inside me, constantly injured with nothing I could do about it, had tipped things over the edge. There was no sports psychologist or anyone I could talk to – not that I would have done anyway. As most footballers do, you put on a front and don't let anyone know how you're truly feeling inside. Bury it all and hope for the best.

You can go a couple of ways with it – but I used to take the self-deprecation approach. You'd get the jokes coming in from staff and players: 'Fucking hell Pipes, if you were a horse you'd have been put down by now.' My nickname at Sunderland became 'Mr Glass', because of Samuel L. Jackson's character in the film *Unbreakable*. 'Have you broken an eyelash this time?' To get by, you end up making those jokes before other people do. I became that guy. But when you come away from the training ground, there's no lower point if you're injured.

You think you're never going to get back fit, and when you do, you know it's going to be short-lived. *Oh my God, it's happened again.* Then the jokes continue. They're trying to have a laugh with you, but they don't realise that every 'Mr Glass' joke kills you a little bit more inside each time.

Injuries ruined my career way before I ended it – they took the joy, confidence and belief in my own ability away from me. They injured my mind way more than they injured my body.

I honestly believe things would have improved if I had been constantly playing and doing well, like in those carefree early days at Leicester City. Everything seemed so easy then. But after my breakthrough season of 2001/02 at Filbert Street, the most games I ever played on the bounce was nine, in my first season at Sunderland. After that? No more than three, for over three years.

There was a pattern at both clubs. Yes, I was nervous before playing, but to nowhere near the same level as those feelings would affect me later on. It was no coincidence that I played my best football then, when I wasn't facing months out of action every few matches.

Brendan Rodgers often talks about dealing with pressure in a routine – the reality is that you have to at a high level. But it's also very difficult to achieve when you can't string a run of games together. Routine is built from consistency.

Those worries and stresses kept me in a disabling state of mind. When you're not sure whether you can even make it through the next game, you start to dread the games you get fit for. I began to fear the build-up to any game.

My best times were the night after I'd played well – it was what I thought being a footballer would be like all the time. For that night, and that night only, I used to think it was the best job in the world. And that was it: straight on to preparing for the next match; straight on to preparing for an inevitable disaster.

The dread evaporated more or less as soon as the first whistle went, every time. You knew then that if you were having a bad game, you were having a bad game – nobody was going to snipe you down from the crowd because of it. How I felt also annoyed me – I knew the nerves would vanish, yet I'd still be paralysed by them beforehand. I just didn't want to let anyone down.

There was someone else I played with at Sunderland who went through something similar with injuries, but was more honest about it than I was. I even remember thinking at the time: *my word mate, are you not intelligent enough to know you shouldn't admit that?* He said he was down, depressed; that his head wasn't right. At that point, I thought *I* was the stronger one for keeping it all inside and just trying to put on a brave face. He asked for time off, but the club told him that they wouldn't pay him anymore. He went back home anyway, though, and we didn't see him for ages. The Sunderland crowd could be harsh, but internally it could be, too: I remember the murmurings with staff and other players that basically said, 'He hasn't got it upstairs.' It was unfair, and a massive shame.

I'm sure some players – both current and former – feel like this now, even if they wouldn't like to admit it. A lot of them love reading *The Chimp Paradox* by Steve Peters, for example, which I think shows you that this kind of thing is happening to more of them; almost as a way of validating their feelings. As you get older, you realise that you can't have been the only one. Niall Quinn told me recently that even he struggled to deal with stuff as a seasoned pro and Sunderland legend. Apparently, he used visualisation techniques to take himself back to carefree football, helping him to manage the nerves and pressure.

I still justify quitting football when I did, because my knees have gone again even now; my surgeon, Dr Richard Steadman, told me that they would before I was 40. It's still a way to protect myself, to think that I didn't just throw my football career away. Of course, there will always be that thought of unfinished business – there was a lot of potential there once upon a time. But if I'm being raw and totally honest? I could have carried on. The idea of taking that load off my mind won out, though, and it wasn't even close. After a string of ridiculous injuries, I went back to Sunderland and played the 'poor me' card. In reality, I wasn't bothered one bit.

I've now reached a point in my life where I know what I did, and what I achieved. Now it's time to just tell the story. Exactly how it was – with everything that happened next. If people think less of me because of it, that's fine. But here it is.

Everything.

CHAPTER 1

Rock bottom

IT'S A good job that I'm not conscious – I wouldn't want to hear what they are saying about me. To be honest, I wouldn't even understand them: what does being sectioned even mean?

As I eventually begin to drift in and out, the only thing I know is that my mum is having none of that talk from the doctor. Most things are a dull fuzz, as I lie on the hospital bed feeling like death barely warmed up, my body a broken shell of toxins from booze and too many pills.

I don't remember much about waking up that day, but it doesn't matter – I almost hadn't at all. This was rock bottom.

When you come out of professional football at 24 years old, it's exciting at first. Money in the bank; freedom; no injuries. You could do *anything*. You don't know what, but you're sure that you'll find your calling in time. *Something* will come along. Won't it?

When you're still asking yourself that question after two years because you haven't found anything you want to do, it's not exciting anymore. It's panic. Your money is running out, and you have no idea where to turn next. No prospects … no hope.

Nights out are fun at first, not least when you're having them twice a week. Then Monday comes around – boring, hopeless Monday. Everybody else is at work. Might as well get the juices flowing with a little tipple. *Is it 12 o'clock yet? It's always 12 o'clock somewhere.* Tuesday, Wednesday, Thursday, Friday – they're all the same. Soon, you're having parties in the living room with your dog, and the reason to get up every day is *Jeremy Kyle* washed down with two litres of whisky.

Soon, you start to feel depressed about that, so you turn to Valium and ease all of those fears away. Soon, you start to worry that what you're doing isn't healthy, so you roll up a joint and smooth it all over in your mind. Soon, you become a person that you and everyone close to you begins to hate – but you don't stop. You can't: you're not ready to. Bell's and *The Real Housewives of New York City* – they're the things worth getting up for every day now.

Soon, you end up doing something stupid – or in my case, lots of things – and it almost costs you everything. But when you've hit the bottom and are still alive to tell the tale, the only way is up.

I want to tell you my story in full now, because I hope it will help others out there who are struggling with their own issues. I know what it's like to be in a place of complete despair, but I'm so happy to say that I have come through those dark days and reached a place in my life where I am happier than ever before. People think I'm mad when I say that these days, having first played in the Premiership when I was 20 – but it's absolutely true.

Football wasn't kind to me as a player, and neither were the years afterwards. But life has given me everything I could have ever wanted since then – I've just achieved dreams of a different kind. I have an incredible wife, and between us we have four unbelievable children who I am grateful for every single day.

In September 2017, I co-founded the FSD Academy in Leicester; an idea that first formed when I was getting the help I needed at Sporting Chance, and that has rewarded me in ways beyond anything I could have ever hoped for. As a result, I'm not writing this book to sell cheap stories – all the profits will go to those two organisations which saved my life in different ways.

So now *this* is my story: the football-mad kid on the streets of Leicester who played in the top flight for his local team and somehow earned a place in club history; the injuries that ruined life at Sunderland and crazy dressing-room tales in between; life after football, with the truth about those horrors which came next.

This is what it's like to be a professional footballer when things don't go right – but most importantly, it's also a story of hope.

CHAPTER 2

Can I kick it?

'SHEAAAREEEEEEEEER!'

Time stopped for a second. The volley was beautiful as it flew through the air, soaring through the sky like a bullet en route to its final destination: the goal. But there was no such thing as nets for me and my brother in our back garden … the ball had to end up *somewhere*. But please, if there is a god, not *there*.

In our house on Sudeley Avenue, we lived next door to a lovely Sikh family who had a couple of lads called Rushpal and Pritpal, with the same age difference as Dan and I. Both were a bit older than us, but we used to play with them a lot out on the street – they weren't very good at football, so I'd regularly rip the older one, who was four years older than me.

I wish I could say it was a few nutmegs that caused a dispute between the families, but it wasn't. We'd always got on with them, although these were different times in 1980s Leicester, when cultures blended on the street but there was suspicion between families who were different.

When the older lad was celebrating a big birthday, several family members flew in from all over and the street was packed for what felt like days as people flocked in and out of the house with food – his mum had been cracking on in the kitchen all week.

Back to that volley. Remember its beauty as it's beating Dan all ends up, flying through the gap between our two houses that we called the goal. Flying directly towards our neighbours' kitchen window, which wasn't double-glazed. Stopping somewhere inside said kitchen, after garnishing a freshly made biryani with broken glass.

Please, no. I heard the screams, but sprinted into the house and hid under my bed. My brother raced up there, lying next to me.

'Please say it was you ...'

I begged him. My mum shouted up. The next-door neighbour was going fucking nuts – there was glass everywhere. My dad went outside, so did their dad, and everybody was furious. Things got heated. I've got no idea whether the poor lad's birthday was ruined for good after that, but I felt terrible – the next day, Mum made me go around and apologise. Thankfully, the neighbour was lovely about it. It was the first time football had got me into trouble.

Dan and I were a nightmare for our neighbours – we had a long back garden with loads of space, but if the ball went over the other fence, you'd have to contend with a grumpy old boy called Len. He was actually a really nice bloke, but just loved his garden; we'd be there ruining his plants in our fun, not giving a shit at the time. It's no wonder he went ballistic. I remember running in the house to tell Dad that he was kicking off, so he'd go out there and hammer him.

'He's going to be a professional footballer … just throw the bloody ball back,' he'd tell him.

I used to feel proud that he'd say stuff like that. With my dad, you knew you were loved not necessarily through the affection he showed – because there wasn't much – but through how hard he would fight for you.

In winter, my brother and I would play with a pair of rolled-up socks and use the doorway as a goal. I lost count of the things I smashed in the living room back then, or how many times I pissed Dad off running in front of the telly during an important game. But he never stopped us playing. I think back to times like that and think he must have just loved to see it; us calling out Ian Wright's name as we fired socks around the room. Dad was a huge Arsenal fan, after all.

My brother, bless him, was always in goal – I'd never let him do anything else. I've got 18 months on him, I was a striker, and *I* was going to be the professional footballer – he needed to help me. Shocking, really. Now he's a brilliant player and turns out for the Leicester Legends with me sometimes – it's a running joke that the manager calls him before me. Dan had trials at Leicester when he was a kid, but his heart was never really in being a goalkeeper, no matter how much I forced him.

Football meant everything to me. You know those kids who just love balls? They're like dogs – anywhere you have one, they'll just follow it with their eyes; if you throw one, they'll go in a straight line towards it. That was me. Every Christmas, from the age of five or six, a ball wrapped up would be my number one present – it didn't matter whether there was a bike hiding behind the curtain or not. It's a cliché, but I genuinely used to sleep with a ball at night. We'd play out on the streets every evening, what felt like hundreds of us, just going for it. There was a game called '60 seconds' where you had to finish with a header or volley – if you didn't, or the keeper caught it, you had to go in goal. I never went in goal. I used to love letting the timer creep to 57 or 58 seconds, putting the pressure on myself to finish.

It was always football, and only football, although Dan and I did have a phase of fishing for one summer in Groby. I've honestly got no idea why – and I remember everyone else wondering why two inner-city black lads were doing it, as well.

My dad liked cricket but absolutely adored football; he was a good player himself, having originally come over to

England from Montserrat when he was a child, kicking about on the streets of London. Later, he became a well-known and respected referee in Leicestershire. He's the sort of bloke who would watch any game on the TV, whether it's Manchester United or Accrington Stanley playing Rochdale in the FA Cup. He told me that he'd had trials for Tottenham growing up, but had always supported Arsenal and used to sneak into Highbury when he was a kid. I never knew whether the stuff about trials was true or not.

Later, Mum would tell me stories of when I was first walking; my old man putting a ball on the ground, only for me to just keep picking it up. After weeks of trying, he came back into the house, annoyed.

'He's never going to be a footballer ...'

At the same time, though, my mum was playing for a women's team in Leicester. So then she'd take over in the garden, and later, I started to kick it properly. I didn't love playing at first, but she was trying to teach me stuff and put the time in. She was the one who persisted with me – and I began to learn.

My first true memory of football was at my primary school in Beaumont Leys, called Wolsey House. They had a team, and I went for a trial when I was about six. The PE teacher at the time was a guy called Bob Thomas, who was massively into his football. He came from Hull, and would just talk about it endlessly – he was brilliant. The first time he saw me play, he said to my mum, 'He's got something about him, you know.' She was buzzing, and came home to tell my dad what Mr Thomas had said to her.

Dad began to show a bit more interest from there, but my mum was the one who was running me to school games and taking Dan and I to the park for a kickaround. We'd try to bully Dad into taking us out, but he'd be getting up for work at 5am, then not coming home until 6pm. Being a dad now, I know how hard that would be – but we'd be begging him to take us, and sometimes he would. We couldn't use the artificial pitches at St Margaret's Pastures because there were games going on, but there was a floodlit bit of grass nearby that we'd use instead. It was a massive treat to go down there.

Mr Thomas at Wolsey House also did so much for me. He was the first person to believe in me after my mum, because Dad was grinding at work all the time, so never got to see me in school matches. It was when I was about six or seven that I first started to think, 'Wait, I'm decent at football.' We played against another local school from Beaumont Leys and I was up against the son of a man who managed the under-8s side from The Blackbird pub.

'Does Matt play for a Sunday team?'

'No ...'

'Well, he's got to come and play for me.'

So, at seven, I joined Blackbird. I was a striker who played a bit like Jamie Vardy, hanging off the shoulder and running through to score goals. I was quick, and I could finish; I used to take the corners and even goal-kicks, too. People used to joke that my most famous moment for Blackbird was taking a goal-kick and getting on the end of it. I was there for one season and scored 68 goals.

One memory I do have from that time, though, was also my first racist incident. It taught me a lot at an early age. We were playing against an older team who had this lad I knew from school – he was the year above me, but we didn't like each other. As I was running by everyone in the game, he shouted out to his team-mates.

'CHOP THAT BLACK BASTARD.'

Dad was reffing, but he didn't hear it. I left the ball, turned around and smacked this lad in the face. I'm not normally like that, but what he said brought the anger out of me. My dad sent me off. I was pleading with him and crying, begging him not to.

'Didn't you hear what he called me?'

But he told me it didn't matter – you just couldn't do that. He whipped out that red card and I was gone. It was the only sending-off I ever got, at any level. Afterwards, I remember my mum telling me that racism was going to be a part of my life from there; I just needed to learn how to deal with it.

My school in Beaumont Leys was so multicultural, though, and race was rarely an issue for me. Our next-door neighbours in Leicester were the Sikh family and an older white lady; next to her was a Bangladeshi family;

there were several black families on the street and a couple from Poland as well. There were so many different creeds and religions.

The only major differences were the tiers of relative affluence on the street, among three-bed semis that all looked the same. In the '80s, a lot of the differentiation came with one question: have you got double-glazed windows? There were the 'rich' families who had nicer cars and well-kept lawns, then the poorer ones who 'only' had wooden windows and didn't look after their houses so well. Ours was somewhere in the middle. There was this kid I used to play with up the street, who wasn't the brightest. One day, he came round my house and looked through the window in total shock.

'Oh my God! Your dad's a blackie!' he squealed.

I'm not sure what he was expecting, but little things like that made you start thinking about your background fairly early in life. Being mixed race has its own challenges sometimes, but to society, I'm black. I didn't think too much of being called a 'mongrel' when I was at school, but that happened sometimes and clearly came from parents. When I got a bit older, I remember seeing a load of kids in town with 'new breed' tattoos; first-generation mixed-race kids as a result of Windrush.

What happened when I was 14 will never leave me, though. One day, I got on the bus with an acquaintance from school, where I was one of three or four BAME kids in about 1,000. It was quite a leap for me, as an inner-city boy, to be at Rawlins school in Quorn – things were very different there, and that experience definitely helped to shape me into the person I am today. That afternoon, when I got on the bus back to Leicester and went upstairs, there were two lads with cans of beer in their hands who were completely out of it. As soon as I saw them, my head said to me: *do not sit upstairs – they will cause you a problem.* They had eyes on me straight away.

My mum's mentality was saying to swallow my pride and go back downstairs – but my dad's was telling me to go and sit in the free seats ahead of them. So we did; me and this lad from school in my class, called Mark Tunnicliffe. Within seconds, it started.

'You are a fucking disgrace to our world, you black c***,' one of them said to me.

And on it went. They slapped me around the head, so I turned around and asked them what their problem was. Mark and I were both 14; these lads were 19 or 20. They slapped me again, then started hitting Mark as well, calling him a 'nigger lover'. The abuse went on for five minutes or so. But I didn't move. And then Mark stood up.

'I've had enough of this,' he shouted. 'He has done nothing wrong and you're picking on him just because of his skin colour.'

They were laughing in his face, but I looked at this small kid – who I didn't even know that well, by the way

– with absolute admiration. The two lads got off at the next stop, so we gave them both the wanker sign from the back windows.

Sometimes, though, you've just got to quit while you're ahead. This was a bus with a load of school kids on it, so it stopped frequently. Sure enough, they sprinted after it, and I shouted down for the driver not to stop at the next place. But he did – and one of the lads got back on the bus. But he didn't say anything, didn't do anything – he just reached behind and picked up a jumper that he'd left behind, then got off at the next stop. Some bullies just aren't as tough without a mate to back them up.

Some people will read this and think I must have wished I had sat somewhere else – but that's not the case. I'm proud of what we did. We were both scared, but from then on I knew I had a mate in Mark. It only made what happened next even more unfair: a few weeks later, he died in his bed with meningitis. It still kills me to this day. I was crying uncontrollably at his funeral, and my mates didn't really understand why – to them, we weren't good mates. But what Mark did that day will always mean something to me, and he will remain in my thoughts forever because of it.

Unfortunately, my mum and dad had it even worse than I did – they had to put up with all sorts of shit in their early days together. By all accounts, Mum was a bit of a stunner back in the day – and that made all the difference. She'd get blokes coming up and whispering to

her in a pub, 'What are you doing with that nigger?' …
'That's a waste' … 'Beautiful woman like you – what are
you doing with a black geezer?' When she was at work,
somebody even kept putting National Front pamphlets
into her desk drawer.

Dad was playing football before us kids were born.
Mum says she used to watch him every now and again if
she wasn't working on a Saturday afternoon, but remembers
that a lot of teams used to single him out for special
treatment because of his skin colour. One time, his team
were playing out in the sticks of Leicestershire and the
abuse was particularly bad from the crowd – he was getting
it all over the place as he ran down the wing. Then it got
much worse: a banana hit him in the face while he had the
ball at his feet.

As people in the crowd were laughing and joking, he
lost it – Dad hopped over the railings and proceeded to
beat the shit out of the bloke who'd chucked it at him. His
abuser was screaming on the floor as punches and studs
rained down on him, and all my mum can remember of it
is an old man waving his walking stick at him, screaming
that he was an animal. It's the last time she ever went to
see him play – she couldn't cope with the behaviour from
either them or him. Nothing happened to the bloke he
beat up, but my old man got banned from playing in the
Leicestershire league for the rest of the season – a good
four or five months.

As I was growing up, Mum drip-fed me stories like these, and I started to wonder: what character was I going to be in this world?

CHAPTER 3

My old man said

MY FAMILY is … complicated.

If I told you that I thought my half-brother was my uncle until I was ten years old, you're just about scratching the surface. And if I said that same man was part of the biggest first-class batting innings in cricket history? But we'll get to that.

First, I want to tell you about my dad, who could easily write a fascinating book about his own life if he ever wanted to.

He was born in Montserrat, the West Indies, and was brought up in a certain way. His mum and dad split up when he was very young, but his old man had never been around anyway – a fair-weather type who didn't look out for his son. So when my grandma decided that she wanted a better life for herself and my dad, she went to find work on another Caribbean island, and had to leave him behind with his aunt when he was only six months old. She returned with a new man – who would later be known to me as Uncle John – and moved to England one year later … again, without my dad. She didn't want to risk not being able to put food on the table, and it was two more years before she'd set up home, got a secure job, earned enough to put a deposit down on a house and been able to send for him. He wasn't able to see her through all of those important years.

From what I've been told by him and others, though, the iron hand ruled. If you were out of line, you were getting clapped. If you didn't have dinner on the table for your parents when they got in – from a very young age – you were getting beaten. The discipline was fierce. By the time my dad came to London, aged six, he arrived at his new home in a new country with a father figure he hadn't grown up alongside. So there he was in the capital, this wild little West Indian boy who'd been climbing mango trees in the mornings with no education behind him – it must have been incredibly difficult for him.

He developed a temper of his own. It meant he got into a bit of trouble in London when he was older, moving on the streets and doing stuff he shouldn't have – getting in with the wrong crowd, basically. He ended up going to a juvenile prison for a few months when he was young, after hanging around with an older criminal – one who was apparently very well known in north London at the time, and would often get him to do his dirty work. He told me once that they'd often see the Kray twins drive by, and that his 'associate' would tell him, 'That's where we're trying to be.'

But it wasn't where he wanted to go. He knew he needed to get out of London, but met a woman who he was with for a little while. She got pregnant, and they had a son – my half-brother Keith, who is 12 years older than me. My dad headed for Leicester to find work, though, and Keith's mum was struggling to cope while he wasn't around. That's when my grandma and Uncle John stepped in: they took Keith in from a young age, essentially raising him as their own.

When my dad moved up to Leicester and met my mum, Keith had gotten used to living where he was and my grandma wanted him to stay. Ten years later, I came along – then, 18 months after that, my brother Dan did.

I grew up in two worlds, really: at home, I was mainly around my mum's white side of the family, who were very close-knit and always showed us plenty of affection. They didn't have a lot, but it was about far more than that: Nan and 'Dandy' – so called because of my oldest cousin's attempt at 'grandad', which stuck ever since – built a family on love. Dandy was one of the nicest people I've ever known; as kids, we'd stay with my mum's parents in Rowlatts Hill throughout the summer holidays and he was the kind of grandad who built you a go-kart from scratch, or swords for Dan and I to play with one another.

Our trips to London for visits with my dad's side of the family were very different. We'd visit my grandma and the man I basically considered my grandad, Uncle John, probably once a month or so in Tottenham. Grandma and Uncle John were very strict and strong people who didn't take any messing, but they were also brilliant with us. It was a different kind of love to what I was used to from my mum's side of the family, which was more affectionate. There weren't really hugs in that house – it was more like a pat on the head, with a 'sit down and behave'. But they made amazing food, and I loved visiting to see that different side of my culture; the music, their values. It gave me an insight into why my dad was the way he was. You imagine being ten years old and expected to do so much for your parents, in fear of getting battered if you didn't.

Grandma and Uncle John had worked hard to get themselves a terraced house in Seven Sisters, where there was only a toilet downstairs. If we woke up in the night needing to go, we had to use a rusty old metal bedpan instead. They were also deeply religious: in the room we stayed, there was a picture of Jesus on the wall with piercing blue eyes. It used to scare the shit out of me – it was like the eyes were following you around the room.

My grandma used to look exactly like my dad, only with glasses and hair like Hamza Choudhury's – her barnet was absolutely huge. I couldn't work out how she managed to keep it so nice, until one day she scratched her head and the wig came off.

We'd always see my half-brother Keith around, but nobody told us who he really was – and to be honest, I never really questioned it. Somebody must have mentioned something about him being our uncle a few times, but I didn't think twice about it. Once I'd found out that Keith was actually my brother, he was playing first-class cricket for Warwickshire.

On Tuesday, 6 June 1994, he also played a major role in his sport's history at Edgbaston. Every cricket fan knows about Brian Lara's unbeaten 501 for Warwickshire against Durham – but it's easily forgotten that you also need someone in at the other end to stick around long enough and help make it happen. Keith was with Lara at the crease that day, finishing with 116 not out himself after a 322-run partnership that set a fifth-wicket county record. It was mad.

Keith was always a party boy – even as a teenager, I could tell he was the life and soul of every gathering. He was loud, drove crazy-coloured cars, and would do daft things like shave his eyebrows off for £200 from his team-mates – just because they'd dared him to. Do you realise how weird someone looks without their eyebrows? I remember watching him at a game once, staring at him for ages trying to work out what he'd done. At the time, I thought he must be a millionaire; on TV, going away with England A and driving around in his sponsored, top-end cars.

'Bruv,' he said, 'if they're giving me £200, those eyebrows are going.'

That's when I realised: *shit, cricketers don't make that much money, do they?* He introduced Dan and I to his team-mates as his little brothers. So there we were, in the Warwickshire dressing room, shaking hands with Lara. As if life hadn't already started weirdly enough.

Mum and Dad were both grafters who made sure we had what we needed in life, even though we didn't have a lot – I remember the times when we had bailiffs knocking on our door. Eventually, my dad set up business on his own as a fabric cutter, while Mum worked with him doing the accounts and would also be out of the house for long hours.

Dad was fiercely protective of his family. When I was 10 or 11 years old, I was playing a game for Beaumont Town against Aylestone Park. It was always our biggest game of the season: they all hated us, and we hated them. I was our best player, but they had this defender who I hated coming up against because he was quick enough to keep up with me. He used to be dirty as well – and in one game, he absolutely smashed me. My dad ran on to the pitch, got this kid by the arm and bawled at him to get his dad. This big guy soon joined.

'What are you going to do?' the lad's old man asked.

My dad resisted his natural urge to smack him, but they argued until things calmed down. Then he said to the guy,

'This lad is going to play at the highest level. Your kid ever puts in a tackle like that again …'

That's how he showed us all love – through protection. If anyone ever stepped up wrongly against any of us, he was like a lion protecting his cubs.

There was this big mixed-race lad who lived near our house, about 18 years old with tattoos all over him. He was a known face around the streets as a drug dealer, who used to show me and my brother a knife in his pocket and say things like, 'If anyone messes with you lads …'

We used to be shit-scared of him. One winter, after it had been snowing, he and his mates grabbed Dan and I for a joke, hung us by our legs and started dipping us in and out of the snow. It was right outside our house, though, so my old man came out of the house and proceeded to reduce this lad I'd thought was hard to a quivering, three-year-old kid within seconds. He came out with a hammer, got him up by the fence and started smashing out panels around his head, screaming for him to never touch his kids again. Funnily enough, he never did after that.

My dad's temper got the best of him at times, but he also taught me and my brother about respect. From a very early age, he'd make sure that when we went around friends' houses, we'd meet their families and say thank you for having us. He'd want us to shake people's hands and say our prayers before dinner. They were good morals, it was just the way he enforced them. But all of those experiences shaped me.

At times it was tough, because my mum was very different – I remember them arguing about each other being too soft or too rough. Don't get me wrong, I didn't get abused, but I think everyone knows that a West Indian family in the '80s could be quite tough. You'd get slapped, hit, the belt – none of this, 'Go and sit on the step for five minutes to calm down.' People would be horrified nowadays with that kind of discipline, but I think that's just the way that the world has evolved. Back then, I don't think some people knew any different. I don't think it did us any harm.

Up until the age of seven or so, I had a very happy childhood. I was playing football and doing well; had a dad who grafted, and a brilliant mum who was loving. They just wanted and did everything for my brother and me.

Then life changed. Dad wasn't living at the house anymore – Mum had kicked him out. I'd never seen him drunk before, but one day he came back staggering up the road. I was sitting in the bay window and called mum to tell her. I was quite a defiant little boy, so when she was telling me to come away from the window and ignore him, I couldn't help myself. I was peeping through the net curtains as he banged on the panes, laughing at him.

'Mum says you can't come in until you sober up.'

He was telling me that he loved me, to let him in the house. But he was absolutely steaming.

'You tell your mum – if she doesn't open the door in two minutes, I'm coming through it.'

I didn't understand what he meant. I definitely didn't take it seriously. In that house, we had a door with a big stained-glass panel at the top of it. The bottom was wood.

He staggered over to the other side of the street, leant on a neighbour's wall – and then took off towards the house. I was watching it all from the front row, open-mouthed.

Oh my God, he's going to jump through the door ...

... BOOM!

There was a massive smash. Glass everywhere. He'd only gone full Superman through the window – and instantly regretted it, as he grunted and rolled around on the floor. I ran into the hallway, where he was surrounded by glass. Blood was pissing out of his arm where he'd sliced it to bits, so a neighbour tried to stem it with a tea towel and put him in the recovery position. I was mesmerised.

There must have been some stuff going on at the time – my brother and I didn't know the extent of it. But the next thing we knew, Dan and I were living with Mum in a big community house for women and their kids in Derby.

What do I remember of that place? That it was a fucking shithole. It was awful. We were living there surrounded by all these strangers and what seemed like hundreds of kids, not really knowing why. We were there for almost a year, but it felt like ages. I hated Derby. We were living in a bedsit, all of us in one room with a communal bathroom; babies running around with shit everywhere. You can't really forget those things – it was not good.

I'm not sure how long afterwards it was, but Dad eventually managed to speak to Mum without the red mist: she felt isolated from her own parents in Derby and he wanted us to come home. He promised to change his ways. So we went back. Life just resumed.

I still have fond memories of my childhood, and still have a solid relationship with my old man now. I'll always love him – he's my dad.

One thing he never lacked was confidence. One day when he was back at home, all of my mum's sisters and brothers' wives were going to London for a theatre show. Dad offered to drive everyone down there in a minibus for the day, and said he'd show us boys the sights while they went to the theatre. Mum said she wanted to stay with us for a family day out, though, so she did. After dropping everyone off, we got caught up in traffic around the West End and suddenly saw a group of people running; they were clearly following someone. Dad being Dad – a loud, self-assured bloke who'd make you cringe by standing up in front of everyone at a wedding to tell a long joke, even if the punchline was crap – knew who it was.

'AWWIIIIGHT!'

At the time, Michael Barrymore was huge on British television – the Graham Norton of his time. We'd never seen a famous person in our lives before. The streets were packed, but Dad wound down the window to bawl out that catchphrase in his loudest voice. Mum was cringing; my

44

brother was cheering. I didn't know what to think. But then one of Barrymore's bodyguards started sprinting over to the minibus – I thought he was going to try to fill my dad in.

'Listen, he's getting mobbed out here. We've got to go two miles down the road – can we get in with you?'

So Barrymore and his two bodyguards got in, sitting next to me and my brother. He was asking us loads of questions, which we – these starry-eyed, squeaky little kids – were answering with single words. Dad offered to pick him up later as well, which he politely declined. But Barrymore was so outgoing and brilliant with us: a lovely bloke. He took a big old £10 note out and signed it, 'To the Piper family, thanks for the lift' and then gave it to my mum. I'm pretty sure she's still got it somewhere.

That day was brilliant. Dad drove us to Buckingham Palace and knew all of the best spots to park in to attract the attention of Gurkha Guardsmen. If you're in the wrong place, they march up to your car with their guns, don't look at you, then stand at your window.

'Can't park here, sir – move.'

You don't get that in the tourist brochures.

Kids are nurtured by their parents. Dan and I have a wonderful mum who you knew from a young age would travel to the ends of the earth for you. She'd give her time and attention for hours, adding snippets of advice you could always draw on in times of adversity. Dad was tough, and demanded obedience, respect and impeccable manners, but loved his kids and worked hard to provide for them.

To demonstrate my parents' differing values and beliefs, there's no better story to share than that of the Bully Twins. Remember when a kid was given the tag of hardest in school? Well, we had two of them at our primary – huge, identical twins who terrorised kids for years.

Dan and I were similar to them, in only as much as being inseparable. We used to play on the Rally – an old, disused rail track that ran through the centre of Beaumont Leys – and one weekend, built the greatest den you've ever seen using huge, reinforced cardboard pipes from Dad's cutting factory. We were so proud: it had a lockable door, windows, a roof and two separate living quarters for us both. It was perfect.

It's a shame those two lads didn't see it that way. One morning, Dan and I arrived at the Rally early, and brought with us a first guest in Axel the dog – our angry little Jack Russell-Staffordshire Bull Terrier cross. When we got there, though, the den had been smashed to bits. Giggles in the background turned to outright laughter: there were the twins, sitting on bikes and both wearing goggles that made their eyes bulge like bugs on acid.

At first, the rage inside me bubbled like a volcano – there goes my dad – but then came the calming thoughts of Mum: *keep it cool ... they want a reaction so they can justify beating the shit out of you.* I reached for one of the half-severed cardboard pipes and turned back towards the twins, who by then weren't grinning anymore. They threw down their bikes.

'What the fuck are you going to do with that?' one of them demanded.

I tugged on Dan's arm and squared him in behind me.

The twins were still moving towards us, though, all four chubby fists clenched into pink balls. I tried to reason with them, to kindly ask (in a roundabout way) why they'd smashed our pride and joy to bits. As Mum was congratulating me in my head, we'd circled around the twins and were out on to Beaumont Leys Lane. I was still holding up the cardboard pipe like it was a credible defence against these two nuggets.

'Now fuck off you little pricks, and don't ever let us catch you up the Rally again,' one of them barked.

Mum was back again: *well done son, handled that maturely – now turn around and get your kid brother home.* I lowered the pipe, took half a step to turn and … *Dad says to smash it around his thick head.* Before I knew what was happening, a twin was rolling around on his back, squealing like a wounded pig.

So we did the natural thing – ran home in record time to hide in the shed, Axel included. We finally emerged when Mum came home from work a few hours later, unamused with how I'd handled the situation and preaching about how violence wasn't the answer. Then Dad returned later, struggling to hide his approval.

'Good lad! Proud of you.'

I love them both. They were polar opposites, and clearly there were some issues between them that Dan and I were shielded from as kids. They each had their own ways, but I know in my heart that they both just wanted the best for us. Especially where football was concerned.

CHAPTER 4

Ian Wright and umbrellas

ONE DAY, a letter dropped through our letterbox. It had Nottingham Forest's logo at the top of it – they'd been watching me for a while, it said, and wanted me to join their academy.

My dad was absolutely buzzing because a professional club had come in for me; I think my mum – a massive Leicester fan – was gutted it wasn't them.

I'd been poached from Blackbird to play for Beaumont Town's under-9s when I was eight years old – the team's manager had come around our house and everything, telling my mum and dad that he'd been watching me for weeks. He thought that I could play in Division One – and as it turned out, I could: in my first season, I scored 63 more goals playing up front. Not long after that, Forest's letter fell through the door.

At first, they were offering me a six-week trial – but I ended up going for one session, and one session only. Dad had been building up how great it would be in the car, but I was crying all the way to the City Ground, where the club's training dome was. When I got there, I didn't want to get out of the car – I was just so nervous. But then came one of my dad's speeches. 'Listen, son: if I had the talent that you've got at this age, I would have given everything to have a chance like this ... now get out of the car.'

Having dried my tears, I got out. At the time it felt like real courage – but I was late because of it. As I got inside, they were calling players' names out. When they read mine, I said absolutely nothing – I was a really quiet kid anyway, but for some reason I also used to be embarrassed about my surname and thought people might take the piss of it. Eventually, the training session started with them thinking I wasn't even there, but I actually ended up doing pretty well; the nerves quickly disappeared and I enjoyed myself.

But sometimes, little things come along to change the course of your entire life. In the middle of the following week, I got a letter from Leicester City: as it turned out, they also wanted to have a proper look at me. I later found out that a scout called Len Mawby had spotted me playing for Beaumont Town, having previously found other local boys like Emile Heskey and Stefan Oakes for the club.

I don't know whether it was because my mum really wanted me to be there or not, but I went to Leicester for the first time and just immediately felt like it was more within my comfort zone. There were lads I'd been playing with and against there, so I already knew some of the faces. I think I was probably too young to appreciate what it meant at the time, but subconsciously you know it's a big step. I remember feeling the same importance when that coach from Beaumont Town came round our house – but I wasn't nervous going there, just like at Leicester. It was different back then, though: you would play in sporadic showcase games rather than in a league system, and train two nights per week. They were big on telling you to stay where you were enjoying your football at the time, too, so I stuck around at Beaumont Town until I was about 12. Eventually, Leicester took me on with a two-year contract.

It's now a big gym, but back then the club's training facility was this vast indoor dome on the side of the training ground. It wasn't remarkable in any way – the only other thing I remember was that it was absolutely freezing in there.

But it's where everything began for me at Leicester City and where I met some of the club's big characters for the first time. You could clearly tell that academy director David Nish was the boss man – he'd never say much to you, instead he just stood there with his arms crossed. My dad told me that he used to play for England, and I appreciated that. You always wanted to impress when Nish was in the room.

Then there was Neville Hamilton, a Leicester man who used to be a pro at Wolverhampton Wanderers and had to finish early because of a heart problem. There'll be more on him later, but for now I'll just describe him in short as one of the three most influential and special people in my career. Chris Tucker was another great coach at the club, who also knew my dad. He worked for the council in the daytime, cutting the grass and pitches at Abbey Park, before becoming this elite coach by night. Sometimes I'd be there at the park with my mates and see him, then again that evening in an official capacity at Leicester. I liked that. Nev and Tuck were the kind of coaches who showed you that they liked you – but I never got that impression from Nish until I was basically in the first team. He was still a ridiculous player approaching 60, by the way: Nish used to do this thing in the gym where he'd take a crossfield ball from someone, move as if he was going to chest it, duck under, let it hit the wall and then take it into his path. He used to embarrass young players all the time with his skill – it was a joke.

Another coach who was good for my development in those early years was Kevin MacDonald, who'd started his career at Leicester as a player before joining Liverpool in the mid-80s. I used to play up in age groups a lot because I was doing well, and I'd regularly be coached by him. MacDonald was one of the most brutal coaches you could imagine – very old school, and to be blunt, sometimes just a bit horrible. At the time I absolutely fucking hated him, but he was very good for me in an environment where football mattered. Some kids would have called him a bully – and Aston Villa did when they sacked him as head of football development in August 2019 – but the way I looked at it, he gave me a good grounding for what was to come. When you reach first-team level and you're getting hammered, you're more resilient because you've had someone like him from an early age. With these kids now, if you don't find a way to deal with that quickly when football means something, you'll struggle.

He also did something once that I've never seen a coach do before or since. It wasn't long after I'd signed on for Leicester, and we had an under-12 game against Southampton at the training ground: quite a big thing, with family and friends coming to watch, and officials in place. MacDonald was shouting instructions from the sidelines, letting our lads know when things weren't good enough, when one of our centre-backs tried to play out. He lost the ball. Southampton were in a counter-attacking situation, and MacDonald shouted out, 'STOP THE GAME!'

So everybody did. The referee was baffled, but MacDonald said he just couldn't have it, and strolled out on to the pitch to talk to the boy about what he had done. The Southampton bench were livid by this point, telling him that he couldn't just stop a game to have a chat with one of his players. But I remember clearly what he said back to them.

'What are we here for?'

It was absolutely crazy: MacDonald just walked out to coach – not berate – the player in question, telling him why he shouldn't have done what he did. That centre-back ended up doing just fine for himself: Matt Heath later played 60 games for Leicester, before turning out for Coventry, Leeds and Brighton among others.

MacDonald was just honest and would tell you how things were in no uncertain terms. I can't remember him swearing at players, but his demeanour was that of a first-team manager. You'd feel nervous whenever he walked in a room and he was short with his praise; not like the flip side, when you'd get both barrels if something was wrong. But he was important. It stood me in good stead to take criticism and deal with the realities of first-team life later on.

A year later, I had the opposite in Jon Rudkin. I loved him. He was much more like the modern coaches of today: always full of praise, with a lot of good ideas, passionate about his job, and someone who would work with you on an individual level as well as a team. He was an all-round top man. If I had to be really honest, he was probably a bit soft – I don't think he ever raised his voice once, and I don't remember him ever having a go at me. Once you get to 13 or 14, though, kids can see who the manager likes and doesn't. I was always earmarked as Jon's golden child and got banter about it – embarrassing, obviously, because nobody wants that. A lot of it might have just been because of my personality; pretty quiet, and a well-mannered kid who trained hard and never played up. I didn't have much of a personality in the dressing room, though, and wonder if it contributed to my downfall a bit later on. I remember having a laugh with the lads and showing off the real me at times, then shutting up as soon as a coach walked through the door.

When I was a youth team player, I was a ball boy for every match at Filbert Street. The scout Len Mawby was also head of the ball boys, and also used to like me – my dad was just chuffed because he'd get a couple of free tickets to watch games. I remember being nervous even doing that job, standing so close to the crowd and getting to experience that atmosphere early on. It was loud, and they thought it would be good for you. You'd get allocated spots around the ground, but everybody wanted to avoid the away end, as that meant getting abuse even as a 12- or 13-year-old kid. Len gave us instructions: if Leicester were winning, pick the ball up and walk it to the players; if we were drawing or losing, get on with it and do it quickly. Common sense, really.

There are three stories that stick in my mind from those days. Len used to be very kind in allocating the good spots to those who he thought were going to make it, and there was a brilliant player one year older than me called Karl

Brennan. We were playing Chelsea, managed by Glenn Hoddle at the time, and there was a break in play while someone was injured. Hoddle called Karl over, started throwing the ball at him and said to him, 'Come on, then: left-foot volleys … headers …' – basically, giving him a mini coaching session during a game while everybody was watching. Very odd. Some people might have wished it was them, but thank fuck it wasn't me – I'd have been shanking it all over the place.

Another story isn't so amusing. We were playing Millwall and winning; I was at the Family Stand end, to the left of the goal. People were nice there – nobody calling you names you'd never heard before, or telling you to get out of their way. I remember it like it was yesterday. Someone had a shot, and Kevin Poole saved it. You didn't have a stool back then, so I just got up and walked to the ball – taking the piss admittedly, but that's what we'd been told to do. One of their players was sprinting over, calling me a little c***, and someone from the crowd had a pop at him. He wasn't finished, though.

'Give me the ball, you black little bastard.'

I stopped for a second, then threw the ball down towards his feet. That was the first time I suffered racism at a professional football match.

Len also knew that my dad was a massive Gooner, and that my hero was Ian Wright – I was a striker, scoring loads of goals, and played similarly to him when I was a kid. In

November 1994, he'd scored a penalty at Filbert Street, but Arsenal lost 2-1 to Leicester that day. He wasn't happy. Still, I plucked up the courage to go on the pitch at full time and ask him for his autograph. I tugged his shirt, so he turned around and looked at me. More of a glare, really.

'Wrighty, you're my hero – can I have your autograph?'

'No.'

'Please ...'

'Didn't you hear what I said? No.'

So I just stood there like a clown. It killed me. Wrighty: if you ever read this, I'd still love your autograph, please.

My experiences with Leicester–Arsenal matches weren't over after that, though. On 27 August 1997, the two sides played out a 3-3 draw that's since gone down as one of the great games in English football history. I was almost 16 then, so no longer a ball boy, but all of the academy players and Foxy Ladies cheerleaders used to sit in the upper tier of the Double Decker during first-team games. I used to love it up there. Our families would sit with us in that section too.

I won't lie: when Dennis Bergkamp scored that first goal of his hat-trick, I stood up and applauded. I knew in that second it was the best goal I'd ever seen live at a football match, and the best I probably ever would see. I was wearing a Leicester tracksuit, though, and it was out of character. One guy about seven or eight rows away took particular exception to it, and started screaming at me to sit down, shouting his mouth off. He was going nuts. Steve Walsh ended up scoring an injury-time equaliser in a mad game. I was cheering it with everyone else, but then all of a sudden I saw this bloke coming at me. Foxy Ladies were getting scattered everywhere … and then he clocked me right on my chin.

So there I was, 15 years old and somewhere down in a footwell at Filbert Street. And then I saw it over the top of me – this giant golf umbrella which rained down from above, cracking this guy square on the forehead and sending him cascading back to where he had come from. There was my dad, standing there with my mum and brother, absolutely livid. It was carnage. Both blokes disappeared out of the ground, and a few minutes later Dad came back absolutely blowing: despite his best efforts, he hadn't been able to catch the other man. On the pitch, my old hero Wright was having a good scuffle of his own with Walshy.

In Leicester's academy, meanwhile, I was developing well. It was a brilliant place to be as a young kid, learning your way through life, not least because of the brilliant coaches that the club had there helping us.

Nev Hamilton was my favourite. He'd originally made it as a pro at Leicester in the late-70s, but Wolves went on to sign him in 1984. Nev was a brilliant, tricky little winger, but he had a heart attack during pre-season and never actually got to play for them. His life was saved, but the doctors told him that he had to stop playing football.

I first met him when I was seven or eight years old, while he was doing sessions for Leicester in the Community. He would see me, my mum and brother while we were out on those evenings at St Margaret's Pastures and love that we were grafting as a family like that. He started coaching me later on, and I loved him. His own dad used to serve the teas to parents at youth team games.

Nev had a pacemaker fitted while he was coaching, and we'd often take the piss out of him for it – as daft lads we didn't really understand what it was, but knew he was fine and happy so it all seemed OK. He'd join in with training and was still unbelievable in his mid-40s against fit, strong young lads – and he'd go all out to win, too.

Nev taught me my favourite move. Even when I made it into the Premiership, I loved the stepover – single, double, the fake back inside. He used to drill it into me for hours; I'd stay behind after training to do it and he'd be on at me.

'Pipes, let's get on the stepovers.'

It was said, jokingly, that I was one of the best stepover merchants Leicester had ever seen – but I would never be as good as Neville Hamilton. That's how good he was.

After I had to stop playing, Nev passed me on my first coaching course. I could start crying thinking about him now, to be honest. When I walk my dog, I often visit the graveyard where he's buried and give him a salute.

Nev is the source of one of my biggest regrets in life. He died in February 2009, when I was going through my bad times. I was drunk at his funeral. Everyone was there – Gary Lineker, Emile Heskey, basically the royalty of Leicester football – and there I was, pissed in a corner. It was shocking.

He had been in hospital because something had gone wrong with his pacemaker. I was coaching at Leicester back then and his dad was still serving the teas. We had a home game one day, and he told me about the illness. Nev had spoken about me and was only down the road from where I lived, at Glenfield Hospital. I said I'd go and see him, but I didn't realise how serious his situation actually was. A week went by, then two, and I was drinking all the time – my life was a mess and only getting worse at that point. I didn't want Nev to see me like that. And then I got the phone call to say he had passed away. I felt horrendous – I could have walked there, the hospital was so close – and it only made me drink harder. I was already in a bad way by then, but it really wasn't good for me; I felt like a terrible person. A man who'd done so much for me in life, and I couldn't take 20 minutes out to go and see him. I had thought he was going to be OK.

I'll never forgive myself for that – but in my work now, I always try to carry Nev's spirit with me. I hope he'd be proud of me for what I became, and not who I was back then.

CHAPTER 5

Fix up, look sharp

WHEN YOU'RE a young footballer, stepping up to play for the youth team is a rite of passage that most players look forward to – after all, plenty of them don't ever get that chance before they're just cut adrift into the world.

My first opportunity with Leicester City's under-18s, though, was yet another invitation for the ground to swallow me up whole. I'll always remember it vividly, because I practically shat myself.

I'd been playing for the under-15s and doing really well against some top teams – it was about this sort of time that they were trying to convert me to being a winger, but I was still scoring regularly. And they were good goals, too. David Nish was always in the background, muttering the odd thing and then disappearing. I remember going to training one Thursday night, though, and one of the coaches said they had some big news for me.

'David wants you to report for the youth team on Saturday.'

A *proper* game – but I'd only just turned 15. People were saying that I was too young and wasn't ready. The under-16s we had back then were already a very good side, and above them you had the full-time youth footballers. And they were choosing me?

On the day of the game, my dad told me to have a nip of brandy to take the edge off my worries. 'It won't make you drunk, just a little thimble …'

I didn't have any, but I was ridiculously nervous. I didn't even know what to wear. All of the youth team lads had Leicester tracksuits, but I didn't.

'You can never go wrong with a suit and tie, son,' my dad said.

Good joke.

'You're wearing a suit and tie.'

I didn't have a suit and tie.

'Wear mine.'

Funnily enough, it looked exactly like you'd imagine a 15-year-old wearing his dad's gear would. I was quite tall but wasn't built like him, so just stood there looking horrified in the mirror; arms too long, legs too wide, shoulders popping out all over the place. It looked like I was in fancy dress. But my dad thought Nish would like it.

As we drove down, I was getting even more nervous. Dad said he'd rung Nev Hamilton, who had told him that the other players were also wearing suits today – it was a big game. They'd asked me to get there a bit later on purpose and the changing room door was shut when I arrived. I was bricking it.

So, the door opened ... and they were all wearing trackies. Every single one of them. Luckily, though, some of the players did actually know who I was already. For some reason, Brian Little, the former manager, had once been on Sky TV talking about the club and how Leicester were proud of their academy with players like Emile Heskey and Stefan Oakes coming through. And, he said, there was another, younger player who the coaches particularly had their eyes on – a lad called Matthew Piper. I couldn't believe it.

So, I was in this dressing room full of older lads who were all trying to fight back the laughs. Guy Branston, the captain, stood up and told them all to shut up.

'Come here, big man – what's your name?'

So I told him.

'The referee's son? Good lad – come and sit by me.'

I only got 15 minutes at the end of the game, but I remember thinking that I'd never be good or quick enough to play this standard of football. I felt way out of my depth. I didn't know who to track, and when I got the ball I just kept it simple.

Gradually, though, as I started playing a few more games, I began to get used to the pace and understanding that I needed for playing at that level. I grew in confidence, improved, and Nish seemed happy with my progress. Happy days. After one more year at school, I was in the youth team every week.

In that period of my life, 14 to 16 years old, I was totally and utterly dedicated to making it as a professional footballer one day. It's the period of your life when you're starting to fancy girls, but the only times my mates had the courage to let girls know that they liked them was at parties. I didn't go to any of them, and it became a bit of a thing in the school – between girls and lads – that it was because I couldn't dance. I used to hate that going around, not least because it wasn't true – I was a brilliant dancer! I just wanted to be a footballer that much. You might have ten other lads who were in the same position as me, but they would go to these parties and experiment with the odd beer. I wanted to be better than them.

Throughout that period there was no drinking, no smoking, no funny business with girls behind the bike sheds. Whether it was the best party of the year or not, I wouldn't be there – instead, I'd be standing in my room like an absolute dweeb, shirt on and everything, dancing in front of the mirror. There might have been ten of those events every year, but I didn't go to one. The day after at school was always the worst, when people were talking about it and you felt left out, especially when one of your mates had kissed a girl who you liked.

I think half of that mentality was about trying to make my dad admire my decisions – if he hadn't been there, I might have gone. The main part of me just wanted football more, though, and it was the same part that loved getting praise from my old man when I'd chosen my potential career over going out. I liked hearing that.

Around that time, my school team was playing in an England-wide tournament where the winners went to Italy. We'd won our Leicester area tournament, and the whole school would come down to watch our games. We had an unbelievable team, with lads at academies for Leicester, Sheffield United and Derby. We wanted to reach the final badly because it was at a pro ground, and we came up against a side from Liverpool in the semis.

We were losing 1-0 at half-time, and my dad came into the dressing room. Our teacher at the time was a rugby specialist, trying to do this uplifting speech, but it wasn't really doing anything. He was never massively into his football. So my dad politely suggested that he sat down, and then took over. Half of me was embarrassed while he was banging on the lockers, but the other half was inspired – it was like an Al Pacino speech.

'DO YOU WANT THIS? DO YOU WANT THIS, LADS?'

In the end, all of the team were absolutely loving it. I equalised with a header in the second half, and edging towards the end of the game it was 2-2. But then came the heartbreak. Their best player was their best player by a mile; he went around a few of our lads and lashed one in from the edge of the box, straight into the top corner. It killed us – we'd taken three busloads of kids and teachers, who were all there with banners. We didn't find out until years later that the lad who'd ruined the afternoon was an up-and-comer called Kevin Nolan. Fair enough, really.

Around that time at Leicester, I looked around the dressing room and thought there were three or four lads who were better than me. For some reason, though, they weren't getting the same chances to play in older age groups as I was. Looking back, maybe the coaches really did just rate me more, though I remember how good some of the other lads were – including one in particular, who I still see locally now. Jamie Aston was a striker, but had the best feet I've ever seen; really quick, and he could finish chances from all sorts of angles. He was intelligent, too: turn, shoot ... goal. The only thing that let him down was that he wasn't very quick.

Thankfully, it wasn't like that for me – everything was in front of me, so I'd always be taking on players. I knew that my outstanding attribute was pace. We had a good team back then: Matt Heath, Jon Ashton and Jon Stevenson all went on to play for Leicester, while Robert Purdie ended up having a good career in the lower leagues. In my mind I was maybe in the top five lads at the club, but looking back at the coaches' decisions, perhaps I was actually top of my age group.

Either way, I always felt confident that I'd make it – but my dad didn't always believe in me as much around that time. I actually had an England trial for Lilleshall, the national academy, when I was 14, and got down to the last 50 players or so – we did some training and there were a couple of trial games. Before me, Andy Cole, Sol Campbell, Michael Owen, Jamie Carragher, Wes Brown, Nick Barmby and several other great England internationals had passed through Lilleshall, which eventually closed in 1999 so that clubs could focus on their own academies instead.

There was a player with me that day who nobody could get near; ability-wise, he was doing things that made you go home and think, 'Am I ever going to reach that standard?' It was Joe Cole. He'd be doing rainbow flicks over the goalkeeper's head when through on goal one-on-one. It was unbelievable, absolutely stupid how good he was. I remember thinking: *that's the level.* I knew I wasn't going to be as good as him, but if I could stay as close to that as possible, I also knew that I had a chance. Even though Cole had a brilliant career when you look back, in my mind he probably fell short of what he should have done from the kid I saw back then.

My dad thought Lilleshall would be brilliant for me, but I knew my mum – while she never said it – didn't want me to go. Around that time, in July 1996, she'd not long lost her dad – my 'Dandy'. We had gone on holiday with them for a week every summer for six years. In my mum's car there'd be my nan, mum and us boys; my grandad would then follow behind half an hour or so later with all of the suitcases, fishing rods and all of our gear in his battered old Vauxhall Viva. That particular summer looked like being the last time we would go away with them, as I was 14 at that point and Dan was coming up to his 13th birthday. Every year we would pull up to this particular cafe on the way to Great Yarmouth, waiting for grandad to roll in with his tired motor. It became a game to predict when he might show up.

Only this time, he didn't. We'd waited there for an hour and a half, so my mum went to a payphone and rang my dad. He told her that Dandy had suffered a bump in his car, and that we should come home because he was on his way to hospital.

Mum was worried, but she kept it together and rang my dad again for an update halfway home. He said that she needed to call the hospital for an update, so she did – and it was devastating.

'I'm really sorry to have to inform you that your dad has passed away,' the nurse told her.

As it turned out, Dandy had been forced to pull over in his car en route, and was hit by a lorry in the layby. She didn't tell us in the car, but had to drive home the rest of the way with tears in her eyes, knowing that her dad wouldn't be there when she got back. I don't know how she did it. She was absolutely besotted with him, and I can only imagine how much that would have crushed her. The idea of losing her oldest son to Lilleshall so soon after would have been really tough on her. Dan and I were absolutely heartbroken to lose him, too – he'd been such a huge part of both our lives, and we'll always have amazing memories of him.

I definitely didn't want to get into Lilleshall – you stayed in their Shropshire hall during your time there, and I wasn't up for that. Like I said, I was a quiet and shy kid. Naturally, I was incredibly nervous at the trial, and played absolutely awfully. My dad let me know about it in the car on the way home. He was silently fuming at the start, but would turn around every now and again to vent his disapproval. He caned me.

I left it until we were nearly home, and took my chance at some traffic lights.

'I'm not having this anymore,' I wailed, then got out of the car and walked off. He got out with me. My mum was there, my younger brother too – not daring to say anything while we got into it – and I refused to get back in. It was the first time I went back at him – after years of him being on my case and saying when things weren't good enough, I'd just had enough.

Afterwards, back at home, he calmed down. He would always speak to me when he'd had a bit of time – it's not like he was always just having a dig. He'd do this thing where he gritted his teeth while he was talking passionately, and he said something I never let him forget.

'Do you know why you're not going to make it, mate? If anything has ever got in my way in life, I've always moved it out the way.'

There was a spider scurrying across the carpet.

'You see that spider there? I'd kill it to get to where I wanted, if I had to. You won't.'

He told me I didn't like the limelight either, and that to play top-level football, you had to embrace and enjoy that.

What he said stayed with me from then – I honestly believe that I ended up making it because I always had in my mind that I wanted to prove him wrong. It sounds cheesy, but I used to blast 'My Way' by Frank Sinatra and think one day, when I've done what he's not done, I'm going to show him that I did it how I wanted to. I didn't need to stand on any spiders to get there.

Looking back, I think it could have just been his way of motivating me all along. Whatever it was, he'd proved himself as a master motivator. It got the reaction he wanted, didn't it?

At Belvoir Drive, Leicester's training ground, I just carried on doing things my own way – and things were looking up. The manager Martin O'Neill would regularly come and watch me for the youth team before first-team home matches. We'd kick off at 10am, ahead of their games at 3pm, so he would come in early to take a look. I'm not sure that Nish used to like it when the gaffer instructed him to try me in different positions, but he didn't have much choice. I played as a No.10 a lot back then.

You'd spot the gaffer turning up – the other players would whisper around that he'd arrived – but it didn't put me off. I wasn't particularly trying to impress him at that point – I thought I was so far away from being in his thoughts that it didn't matter what I did. Later, though, I got told that he was literally coming just to watch me. Parents spotted it, other players spotted it too, and that's when things began to change.

I didn't get bullied, because my team-mates generally liked me, but once a few beers had gone down I'd be getting called 'the golden child'. It was an uncertain time for a lot of them, who didn't yet know whether they'd be getting a professional deal or not. The difference between that and the scrap heap was big.

'Surely they've put you straight on a pro contract?' they'd ask. I didn't like it, but they would try to push hard and get it out of me. Back then, a youth team contract was for three years: £42.50 per week in the first year, rising to a whopping £47.50 in the second and £90 in the third. Usually, there was no guarantee of what you'd get after that, but mine was a bit different. I signed a normal youth team contract (YTS) for the first year, but then they committed to making me a professional after that with a three-year deal that went up to £150 per week by the second year, and £200 in the third (with another £150 in bonus money if I got into a first-team squad). That was the contract I played on in the Premiership, and later managed to forge my little place in club history.

There are a couple of games from my academy days that I'll never forget. One was against Middlesbrough in my YTS year. I'll do my best to avoid making it sound like a rejected scene from *The Matrix*. We'd got a corner – it was 0-0 I think, quite late on – and I hung around on the edge of the box waiting for a break. Luckily, the ball came to me, I took it on my chest, turned … and then started running. I blew past the first player who tried to engage, then the second and started to see the red shirts flooding back. I knocked it around the third lad, went shoulder-to-shoulder with another, then brought it inside a fifth player when he tried to slide-tackle me. I went to shoot with my right, stopped it as another Boro player slid in, then took it past the keeper and slotted it in. I'm not going to lie to you: it was an unbelievable goal.

Nev Hamilton used to let you know that you were a good player, but he never over-praised you. At the end of that game, though, he booted the door open and got into preacher mode.

'I've seen Julian Joachim! I've seen Emile Heskey! But I have never, *ever* seen a goal like that down this training ground. What a player!'

It was embarrassing, all of the other players just sitting there while he boosted me up. We went out that night, and that's when a lot of them were taking the piss.

The second game I remember well was against Manchester United in the FA Youth Cup. They weren't in our local sector for matches, so we never got to play them normally, but we'd heard that they had an unbelievable team. The game was at Carrington, their training ground, and a few of their first-teamers came to watch.

We were 3-0 down after 20 minutes. As we got to half-time, I'd barely had a touch. We thought Nish was going to boot water bottles around, but he did the complete opposite.

'What can I say, lads? Sometimes in football, you just come up against a team that's better than you. You've just got to take it. Nev, anything to say?'

'Just better than you, lads. Keep trying.'

Obviously, they knew exactly what they were doing. I was never one of the most vocal players, but as I walked back out on to the pitch, I remember thinking: *better than us? Who says that?* So we went into the huddle, where usually I never spoke. But I was pissed off.

'From kick-off, give me the ball,' I said.

Sounds big-time, doesn't it? But they did give me the ball and I started running. I didn't know where I was going, but somehow I managed to make it all the way and score. 3-1. Two minutes before the end we'd dragged it back to 3-3, taking the game to extra time, but then lost it.

It was gutting. But as it turned out, not the end of the world: Martin O'Neill really had been watching me closely.

CHAPTER 6

Living for the City

MARTIN O'NEILL used to put his squad up for first-team matches on a wall at Belvoir Drive.

If you were a reserve and playing well, you might check it every now and again. I think the wider squad was probably around 40-odd players at that time, if you considered first-year pros and second-year pros, most of whom were older than me and never even checked the list because they knew they'd never be on it. If you even got caught having a peek above your station, you'd be hammered for it, so although in the back of my mind I thought I had an outside chance, I didn't dare to look. One Thursday before a game, I went into the dressing room and heard my team-mates chirping away.

'Your name is on the list, Pipes – you're travelling to Newcastle ...'

I thought they were having me on, so I went out and there it was ... me in the 18-man squad for Leicester's trip to St James' Park on 15 April 2000. Eleven players, five subs and two spares to travel up with them. Obviously, I knew I would be in that latter pair – but I couldn't have cared less. I was in.

I rang my mum and dad in the toilets, but was panicking. I didn't know what to do after that, so I just went training with the youth team as usual. David Nish set up without saying a thing to me, but then Steve Walford – O'Neill's trusted first-team coach – strolled out on to the pitch.

'Didn't you see your fucking name on the list?'

'Yeah …'

'So you're fucking with me, Pipes. Over here …'

I left the youth team area, went past a group of lads who were two or three years in front of me, and pitched up with the first team: Steve Walsh, Matt Elliott, Muzzy Izzet, Neil Lennon. And you know what? I was actually good in that very first training session. Because it was a Thursday, the gaffer wasn't there – he'd only come out on Fridays, when we'd have 45 minutes consisting of one-touch five-a-side, two-touch for 10 minutes after that, three-touch for the next 10 minutes, then the last 15 minutes all-in. He used to want it rapid and sharp, with tackles flying in. As long as the intensity was there, he was happy.

By the time of that Newcastle game, I'd got the first-team tracksuit on and had saved up to buy this little Louis Vuitton washbag. All the youth team lads were wishing me luck, and David Nish – who never gave me any praise – poked his head around the door.

'Too soon for you, son …'

I probably thought it myself, to be honest. I look back and realise Nish was unbelievable for me, though; another character who did things his way. It's funny – he used to have a little column in the programme, and that was the first time I realised he liked me. He wrote: 'Matt's got a massive chance and will earn money in football somewhere, without a doubt. We believe it will be at the top level – but it depends on him.'

He never praised me to my face. I remember the first time I answered back to him, and it didn't go well. We were playing at Coventry away and I was starting to believe some of my own hype. Nish used to lean on his umbrella and bark at you if he thought you needed telling something.

'Look at you,' he'd sneer. 'Nev, he thinks he's a player,' then point his umbrella at you. I told Nish to fuck off, and he was livid. He told Nev to substitute me straight away, then had another pop on the bench. I deserved it, obviously. He knew that if he allowed me to become big-time, it'd hurt me as a player in the long run. Don't let him think he's made it, travelling with the first team and getting above his station. I might not have thought it at the time, but looking back, I have a huge amount of respect for Nish and the way he coached me at Leicester.

But I was with the first team on this occasion, and we flew up to Newcastle. O'Neill didn't put me in the squad – it was me and Stefan Oakes who missed out – so we just sat there in our tracksuits while the players got ready to go out.

'Get changed – you're warming up,' the gaffer told us both.

He wanted me to experience the feeling of a big crowd. Oakesey knew I was shitting myself, so purposely suggested a game called 'cricket'. You wouldn't do it warming up for a Premiership game: it's where you pass it to each other but try to bounce the ball just in front of the other person, so the ball skids up off the turf. If your touch isn't tight, you've had it – caught at slip. So he was spinning in balls right in front of the Newcastle fans, and my touch was all over the shop.

'Fuck me,' he said, 'it's a good job you're 18th man, isn't it?'

They let me sit on the bench. Walford got me up mid-game, by the side of the pitch, and told me to pretend that I was out there, to soak up the atmosphere. I got goosebumps. I wanted it.

I never got on the bench under Martin O'Neill – I got injured soon after the Newcastle trip, and six weeks later he joined Celtic to end a major era at the club. I loved him as a manager even from that short time, but there was something I didn't understand at first. I would be questioning myself all the time in those early days of breaking through, but praising myself inside for the good things I'd done in a session. Then we'd be walking off the training pitch and the gaffer would say, 'Hold on, I thought we were supposed to have Pipes training with us today?' He was just having banter, but it got my head down a bit. Now I'm older I see it, but at the time I thought he was caning me.

He commanded such a huge level of respect. There was one game we were losing, and at half-time he gave a speech like the one I remember my dad delivering in that school cup game in Liverpool. Only this was the real thing – hardened pros who'd been there and done it. And he got them pumped – hairs on the back of your neck stuff. I was only in there observing as a youth team player, but I remember the effect it had on the team.

Steve Walsh was coming to the end of his time at Leicester around then, but there was one training session where the team who'd lost the Friday five-a-side would have to run around the training pitches as punishment. O'Neill got one of the quicker players to time it. 'Everyone back here in 30 seconds, otherwise you're going again.'

Walshy jogged around slowly and got back in about 50.

'Back on the line, Walshy.'

He wasn't having it.

'Get back on the fucking line ...'

So he jogged it again.

'We'll be out here all day son, because my will, will beat yours.'

Walshy tried to stay strong – he could have run a marathon with the amount of times he did it in the end, I swear – but O'Neill was always going to be stronger. He finished it.

His coaching staff were brilliant, too. John Robertson was the one who'd pushed for me from the beginning – he used to watch some of my youth team games from the dugout, fag on, giving Nish a few instructions for me. I had no idea he was a European Cup-winning footballing legend in his own right back then – but my dad did, and told me to hang on to his every word. All of the gaffer's coaching team – Robbo, Walford, goalkeeping coach Seamus McDonagh – struck you as old-school Sunday League types who worked in football because they loved it, not because they were trying to revolutionise the game. That's how it came across, and it was good because you didn't feel any added pressure. Obviously you feel nervous when you train with the first team, but when you saw Walford and Robertson smoking on the sidelines, scruffy tracksuit bottoms on, socks all over the place … it was just nice.

It's why I used to hate going away with England Under-21s later in life. If I ever went there, it was all so polished and super professional: 'Control with the inside of your foot, pass.' It felt like that all the time, from the very first trials I ever had with them. At Leicester, the players felt at ease, though training was still professional and the players cared. The coaches didn't really work on patterns of play out from the back or anything like that – the stuff you perceive a top Premier League side to be doing now – but it was fine. Maybe they'd be reminding you to cover the back post and make sure you had a player marked if you were about to play someone like Alan Shearer, but not much more.

That's why O'Neill used to come out on Fridays: that session only lasted about 45 minutes, but he wanted his presence there – people would be nudging each other as if to say, 'The gaffer's coming …' The intensity would go straight up.

The way I look back on him, and the stuff he did for me, he was just a brilliant man-manager. I heard a story once about a Leicester first-teamer who had a particular liking for nights out, but O'Neill had signed him in the first place on the proviso that wherever he lived, the gaffer also had a key for the house. One day, when this player didn't come in – saying he was ill – the gaffer sent Robbo round to check on him and see if he was telling the truth. He wasn't: he was in bed steaming. When the player finally came in, it apparently kicked off and was dealt with in the office. All I'm saying is that I've heard Martin O'Neill could be quite handy when he wanted to be …

He knew the players he had to put an arm around, and knew the others who needed a kick up the arse. In some half-time team talks, Walshy would tell him that he couldn't play another half an hour, and the gaffer would be willing him on in his face.

'Alright gaffer, just another 20 minutes …'

The game would restart and Walshy would know when the time was up, calling to the dugout. But I remember hearing O'Neill talking to Robbo when I was on the bench.

'Don't look at him,' he'd say, then just ignore him. The gaffer used to have this knack of building a player up, getting in their head and then playing dumb when they were begging to come off.

When he took me to Newcastle, I was 18 years old, in an established and achieving Premiership squad littered with talent. I'll always look back and remember that introduction he gave me, and I could never repay it. As it turned out, Leicester couldn't recover when he left to join Celtic in that summer of 2000.

Thankfully, my playing career at that point was looking far more promising than any possible future as a boot boy. I started doing that job when I was around 16, cleaning the boots of Emile Heskey and Pegguy Arphexad. Both were great with me, but Pegguy was particularly brilliant – if only for the fact I did such a shocking job with his boots and he'd still be very generous at Christmas. Kids nowadays would laugh about it, but to me, the £150 that he used to chuck me – a kid who had grown up on the outskirts of town, getting something for basically *not* cleaning boots – was amazing.

My logic was this: Emile was the superstar and I had to make sure that his boots were clean, without fail. Anyone who knows me will tell you that time-keeping is not among my strong points. If training started at 10am, I'd have to be in for 9.30am at the latest to get both sets of boots done. In reality, I would more often get in at 9.50am, sprint up from the bus on Aylestone Road, grab Emile's boots, scrub them quickly and then hand them over with seconds to spare.

Nish wanted the young lads out there ready – 9.59am, no messing. So Pegguy's boots often had to get sacrificed, and this would happen far too regularly. I'd get fined a few quid for my own boots not being clean, and then as I was jogging over to the youth team pitch, I would hear the cry.

'PIIIIIIIIIIIIIIIIPES!'

Even Nish would know what had happened just from that – another fine. Pegguy would come in after training and say to me, 'This is getting stupid now. Come on, man ...'

He'd batter me, but in a jokey way, then at Christmas still be generous with his cash and tell me to have a nice time. His character was just like how he played in goal – laid back and relaxed. I saw him recently, and he was exactly the same.

Emile, meanwhile, used to have a massive Nike deal – and luckily for me, we were the same size. So he'd give me loads of kit – the newest boots, for example – and all of the other youth team lads would be envious. He used to look after me well.

One of my other jobs was looking after the away team dressing room on a matchday at Filbert Street. I was starting to be more aware of life's social aspects by this point, and it brought me out of my shell a bit – I started to get more confident. I wasn't outgoing then, but because I was polite, they'd put me and another lad on looking after the visitors – standing on the door, fetching things for the kitman or players if they needed anything. Leicester had a game against Middlesbrough in 1998, and Paul Gascoigne came out to see me.

'Go upstairs and tell John on the door, "Gazza needs his medicine,"' he said.

I had no idea what he was on about, but it was about half an hour before kick-off. So I went upstairs to see John.

'Gazza needs his medicine.'

He knew exactly what I meant: out came a pint glass, and a generous measure of brandy got blasted into it. This wasn't a thimble like my dad had tried to give me before my first youth team game.

'Don't tell anyone what it is – just take it back down.'

Gazza, who was waiting at the door, took the glass gratefully and chugged it down. On the stroke of half-time, he scored the winner in a 1-0 victory for Boro. It was his first goal in English football since that ridiculous free kick against Arsenal in the 1991 FA Cup semi-final. It wouldn't be the last time that our paths crossed, either – albeit the next time was in very different circumstances.

Leicester's own first-team squad had no shortage of characters back then. Ultimately, Martin O'Neill had built a team of winners – it didn't matter whether you came from the fourth division, top flight, or had been kicked out of another club: you had to have ability, but the gaffer also really valued mentality. Did you want to win? Because he did, every single game, and so did his backroom staff. What you looked like or where you came from just didn't matter.

Sometimes it was chaos, because you had people like Garry Parker, who'd been around the block as a wily operator with several teams. As well as big players like Matty Elliott, Neil Lennon and Muzzy Izzet, there were the likes of Robbie Savage, Gerry Taggart, Frank Sinclair, Andy Impey, Tim Flowers and Stan Collymore – huge characters around that time. I used to love it as a young player, though, having all of these personalities around who did loads of different things to each other.

Parks had a favourite trick. Savage always had the best car in the car park – sometimes a bright yellow Ferrari, the next time maybe a bright red Lamborghini – but Garry used to nick the keys from his pockets, head back out to the car park and drive Sav's car into the gaffer's space. Then the gaffer would come in and have the arse with Robbie, going nuts at him – not the guy who'd parked it.

Another time, Parks hid fish in Sav's car – but not one, two. He'd say to me, 'Never hide one, because then they'll think they've found it.' So he would lift up the back seats and put one under there, then another under the bonnet so it stank when Sav was driving. He used to find that one easily, but would then come in for days saying his car still reeked and he couldn't get rid of the smell. I've got no idea how long it took him to find the other one.

Before a youth team game one hot afternoon, the sprinklers were going on the training ground pitch. Robbie rocked up in his drop-top sports car and said his normal stuff to the young lads like, 'Listen: if you keep working hard, one day you might be able to pull up in a £200k car too.' I thought it was just banter, but a lot of the other youth-teamers didn't like it. Parks saw an opportunity.

'I know how we'll get him back, lads.'

So he waited until Sav had parked up, and turned the sprinklers towards his car. A few minutes later, it was like a swimming pool in his Ferrari.

Later, when I'd established myself among the first-team group a bit more, I went out with some of the players in London – a city where it felt like Frank Sinclair being out was like David Beckham doing the same in Manchester. I don't know if it was just because clubs and bouncers knew him from being on the scene when he was at Chelsea, but he got privileges in some places; you'd see lads like Frank Lampard standing in queues waiting to get in, while our Frank would wave us straight in with him. He was getting us into these clubs where there were about five different queues for various guest lists.

One night, we went to a place called Sugar Reef in Soho – I was drinking and having a good time, but not steaming. I was only a young lad so didn't need that much anyway – a good thing in London, when you're only earning a few hundred quid per week.

During the night, I went downstairs to the urinals a little bit tipsy, keeping my head down. All of a sudden, I saw this bloke standing next to me.

Fucking hell, it's Stevie Wonder.

I couldn't believe it. I must have been staring at him funny for a bit, because an arm came and touched me on the shoulder from behind – his bouncer's – as if to say: *yes, it's Stevie Wonder – now stop looking at him while he's having a piss.* I was so star-struck I hardly said anything.

I shot back upstairs.

'Frankie! You'll never guess who's down there.'

Obviously, none of them believed me. 'I promise you,' I pleaded.

Sure enough, Stevie Wonder came upstairs and everyone went over to him. I'll never forget it: the first thing Frank Sinclair told him was, 'Stevie! Listen – I was *made* to you. My mum and dad had you playing in the background ...'

I think he secretly enjoyed that – it was brilliant.

I hated Christmas time among the squad, though. Some of the older first-team pros would declare that they needed a show putting on by the young lads. You had to rap a

Christmas song, and could do it in twos – so you'd basically just whack the music on and start dancing.

I had to do mine with Jordan Stewart. I get nervous about a lot of things, but for that I was absolutely bricking it for weeks, absolutely petrified. In the canteen, in front of everyone? Literally anything else sounded better. Some of the young lads loved it because they were getting a bit of attention from the first team, so would come up with these hare-brained schemes and get dressed up too.

But we did it – 'O Come All Ye Faithful' is a scar on my memory. Jordan shat it as well, so he just danced, but luckily he could do that like Michael Jackson. So there he was, moonwalking and spinning around while I rapped 'joyful and triumphant'. The first-teamers loved it in the end – if you had a go, they appreciated it.

While there were a lot of jokers and big personalities in that squad, what I loved about them was that they would look after you and pull you out for praise if they thought you had a bit of something about you. They'd give you advice all the time. Muzzy, Matty Elliott and Brian Deane were all good for that, but so too was Stan Collymore – he was genuinely brilliant sometimes.

There was always a 'but' with Stan, though. I met him before I knew about depression and mental illness, and had no idea that he'd been in the Priory for his struggles the year before he'd arrived at Filbert Street. Some days, I would come in and he would say things like, 'How are you, Pipes?! Come and sit with me. How are things going? What are you struggling with at the moment?' He'd ask me some great questions and be incredibly generous with his time.

Then I could go in the very next day, and because he'd been so nice the day before, I would say hello to him in the same way.

'Don't call me "big man" – you're not in the first team yet. You can't talk to me like that.'

He would dress you down. If you were sitting on the treatment table, he could come in and tell you to get the fuck off it because you weren't at that level yet. You never knew, especially as a young lad, where you stood with him. Looking back now I understand why, because he'd gone through a lot of issues around that time – depression, the Ulrika Jonsson incident – and you could see it. Stan could be nasty and cutting at times, then be the most kind and generous bloke with his time.

Honestly, though, I look back on him with very fond memories at Leicester. Even though he could behave badly sometimes, some of the nicer things he did in giving up his time to help me went beyond that – and it wasn't just me, either. His time at the club was fleeting, but he was very good to me at certain points.

One thing I really remember about him happened after he suffered a terrible ankle break in a game against Derby. He twisted it and snapped it like a compound fracture

– it was horrible. Stan demanded a lot from the physios afterwards, a real tunnel-vision approach to getting back fit, and he drove them hard. But the outcome was brilliant: they worked for him, he put in the graft, and then when he got back he bought all of them a Rolex watch each. I remember looking at that and thinking, 'That's class'. I also remember that it surprised me, because sometimes you just didn't know what mood he was going to be in when he arrived on any given day. You expected that gratitude from someone like Muzzy, who was kind all the time, but other people would have looked at Stan – sometimes, I did – and thought he didn't have that kind side to him. But he did.

Unfortunately, he also crossed Trevor Benjamin once – and just about lived to tell the tale …

CHAPTER 7

The adventures of Pipinho

THINGS CHANGED a lot at Leicester City after Martin O'Neill left in the summer of 2000. Peter Taylor was in charge, and I didn't envy his job one bit. Replacing the gaffer was always going to be a near-impossible ask after the success that Leicester had enjoyed under him: days when going to Wembley started to feel like a once-a-season trip for City fans.

On a personal level, things didn't get off to a good start at all. A month into the 2000/01 season, I picked up another knee injury that needed keyhole surgery – but my card had already been marked before that.

I had one year left on my contract when Taylor arrived, but he wasn't having me from the start. I remember a few times in first-team training, Guppy, Lennon and Muzzy especially would tell me, 'Mate, you're decent.' They used to sit on the bank to watch some youth team games and liked what they saw. 'You've got a chance – keep working,' they would say.

I was training hard with the first team and doing well in Taylor's sessions ... or so I thought. I was getting nothing from him – quite literally. He liked Jordan Stewart, Martin Reeves and Matt Heath at that time, and I was more or less fourth in that youth pecking order. All three of those lads had new contracts by January 2001. I didn't have an agent at the time, so my dad was asking me whether he'd done the same for me. Why hadn't he called me into his office yet? I should knock on his door, he said. But I wasn't going to do that.

So I waited. When he finally did call me in, I thought he was going to give me something similar – he was handing all of these new contracts out to my team-mates, upping their wages from about £200 per week to £1,500.

And then he dropped the bombshell.

'I don't see you getting in my first team,' he said. 'Maybe you could go out on loan to a lower division – you're a good winger who can beat a man and get balls into the box, and I can see you at that kind of level. You're potentially a saleable asset for the club. We're Premiership. I know you would have been talking to your mates, but you're not going to get offered what they got. We'll give you a new contract on £375 per week.'

Taylor wasn't actually a bad coach himself, but my initial thoughts were that his training sessions were weak – mostly because he often didn't take them himself. We'd been used to fast and intense five-a-sides under O'Neill and Garry Parker, who by then had retired from playing to become reserve team boss.

In Taylor's first training session, he sat everyone down with his first-team coach Steve Butler – a former striker who'd joined him at Gillingham for the end of his playing career, then at Leicester. But he wasn't an experienced guy. This was pre-season, remember: normally those sessions included a lot of running, getting you ready for the new campaign after you'd been off for a few weeks.

Their favourite activity was something called SkyCam – Taylor loved it. You'd be paired up, someone would do a skill, everyone would watch, and then you'd repeat it in front of everybody. That was it – I used to hate it. Sometimes, a SkyCam would be your partner pinging the ball at you from 30 yards, you would keep it up on your chest, knee it, head it twice, then volley it back. Imagine the pressure, the banter, the bad touches – especially if you were a young lad. Someone firing a ball at you while you were trying to do all of those things, and a lot of people struggled with it.

It was quite boring, and no one was fit – I certainly didn't feel so when we started that season. But amazingly, the team actually got off to quite a good start; by 1 October 2000, they were top of the league. Taylor was a much better coach than he was a manager, and would have made a great

No.2 because he was a very likeable guy. A lot of the players since have said that he would just try to be everyone's mate, and it's true really – I never heard him cane anyone. I think he was too close to the players. One minute he was trying to get on with them all, the next he was having to be their boss. I think there does have to be a barrier there; it can kill a lot of respect straight away, especially after you've just had a man like O'Neill in charge.

People liked Taylor as a bloke – they just didn't think he was a very good manager. But that niceness led to some huge contracts, just to keep players sweet in a big time of change. Muzzy was worth the £35,000 per week he got in the end, and big players like Elliott and Savage also got far bigger deals than they were already on. People couldn't believe it – even young kids like me who didn't really understand the money side of things knew that was big for Leicester City. I'm not saying that those players weren't worth what they got, but some of them probably trebled their salaries from before to compensate for a difficult situation. I didn't know anything at all about the club's financial position at this point, though – and I wasn't really bothered. I was playing for Leicester and enjoying myself.

One player Taylor really didn't get on with from the beginning, however, was Stan Collymore. By October 2000, he was with us in the reserves after being put on the transfer list following a 1-1 draw against Everton the previous month. Taylor had battered him in the press for it, saying he'd put in a performance that was 'unacceptable for a professional footballer', and fined him a week's wages after he didn't turn up for training once. What happened in the reserve game that followed against Charlton basically spelled the end for Stan at Filbert Street.

I wasn't playing in this particular game, as I was recovering from knee surgery, but I watched on from the dugout as he proceeded to play like Zidane. He was playing a bit deeper than usual, as a No.10, and he was absolutely on fire: pulling balls out of the sky, playing people in, executing passes you didn't think he'd seen.

Trevor Benjamin had joined the club from Cambridge United that summer as one of Taylor's new signings, and hadn't yet broken into the matchday squad – at 21, he was still a young lad like me. Trev was great at holding the ball up and bullying people in the box, strong at the back post and with his head, but he was having an off night against Charlton. Stan was playing him in regularly and watching those chances fly out of the stadium – and he wasn't happy about it.

At half-time, the players came off. Trev was in front and overheard some conversation behind him – it was Stan absolutely hammering him in the tunnel. The players who weren't playing filtered in behind, including me, so I heard everything: Stan going in hard on Trev's weight because he knew he'd had some struggles keeping it down, and some other things that I couldn't quite believe were coming out of his mouth. It was all pretty nasty.

Trev must have said something back, and Stan didn't like it – he was the older professional, after all. Everyone else who wasn't playing filed into the changing room quickly, because they knew this one wasn't over. Parks was telling everyone to sit down, but Stan and Trevor were at the far end next to a physio table.

And then things absolutely kicked off. The table got launched, arms started swinging, and the next thing we knew, Stan was on the floor with a bloodied face. Everyone was trying to come between these two huge blokes, nervously – and then I heard the call.

'PIIIIIPES!'

I was standing closest to the door.

'Go and get the manager – he's sitting upstairs.'

So I raced up to grab Taylor, who was in the stands. Before I'd even finished my sentence, he'd burst past me downstairs. In between, it had all kicked off again: Parks had sent Trevor to the physio room to cool off, and Stan had been told to stay in the dressing room. When he got up to leave, Garry stopped him and told him to leave it.

'I'm just going to the toilet, Parks.'

But he didn't: Stan slipped outside and went straight for the physio room. Everyone rushed in afterwards to see the same scenario: Stan on the floor once again, with Trev bouncing over the top of him like he was ready for more.

The moral of that story? Don't fuck with Trevor Benjamin.

If only Sav had got the memo. When Taylor arrived, he'd tried to make his new midfielder feel 10 feet tall in training – understandable as a manager, but I remember standing in one training session where he went a bit too far with it.

'You see this group of players here? Everyone is raving about David Beckham, but we've got a player in the team just as good as him.'

Everyone thought he was going to say Muzzy.

'You see this lad here?' he said, pointing at Robbie, deadly serious. 'His delivery is just as good.' I bet even Sav was embarrassed. When you're hearing that kind of thing a lot, though, you grow in confidence so much that you think you're an absolute baller.

But what started happening in training was that if the ball didn't go straight to Sav's feet, he wouldn't extend himself to reach a misplaced pass. Trev would sometimes take the ball down, pop it out, and maybe sometimes it would be a foot in front of Robbie. He'd let it run.

'Shit ball, Trev …'

Trevor had just been signed for £1m, and since he was a young player like me, he wasn't up in the first-team hierarchy. If Muzzy had played that pass, Robbie would have bust his balls to get there.

'Fucking hell Sav, run on to it,' Trev would say.

'To be honest mate, I was looking at your eyes and you were looking over there.'

Sav used to batter Trevor about his eyesight all the time – apparently, his corneas weren't round, so he couldn't actually see properly.

One day, though, he'd had enough. Trev picked up Robbie and launched him into a row of thorn bushes we had at the training ground. It must have hurt, but everyone was crying with laughter as he crawled out from the bottom with the right arse, his face covered in cuts.

Some massive players left Leicester when Taylor arrived. Stan went to Bradford not long after his scrap with Trevor, following Walshy, Lennon, Tony Cottee, Ian Marshall and more out of the door.

They were the kind of players I had grown up hearing about and watching on the TV, and they then got replaced by the likes of Junior Lewis. Before Leicester signed him from Gillingham, he hadn't even been getting in their first team every week – and that was in the second tier. Players were talking about it, too, not quite believing what was going on.

Taylor signed him and started playing him in central midfield straight away – it was mad. Junior was a top man, a real nice guy, but a Premiership footballer he was not. Lee Marshall came in from Norwich in the same month, playing on the right wing. I looked at him and thought, 'He works hard, but he's getting in this side and you're telling me I'm not good enough to?' That's why I started to think that I could do it. I started to believe that if I could just stick around for long enough, whatever they offered me I knew I'd sign.

Not all of Taylor's signings were bad. Gary Rowell and Callum Davidson were very good players, and Simon Royce was a decent goalkeeper. Trevor would have been far better with a development manager – he was 21 when he came to Leicester, so not the finished article, and going into a team that was losing every week can't have been good for him. I thought he was a good player who just needed some better coaching at that stage of his career.

Ade Akinbiyi had signed for a club-record £5m too, which immediately made his life difficult: you hear about that price tag as a player and think you're going to get a game-changing striker. I'd seen him do well at Wolves before that, scoring goals, and when he got to Leicester he was a beast in training: quick, strong, banging them in all over the place. So when Ade wasn't scoring with that regularity in the first team, it was a big surprise – he was genuinely decent.

I once heard an interview with Ian Wright, who admitted that he was petrified when he signed for Arsenal because it was a club-record fee. Even someone like him, who'd already been scoring in the top flight for Crystal Palace, was terrified about that. And this is what I think happened with Ade: he knew about that price tag, and knew that Taylor had brought him in to score goals. Wright said he knew he had to score within his first three games for Arsenal, because once it went past that, it would strangle him and he'd feel the pressure. In the end, he scored in each of his first four starts. Ade got his first goal in his fourth game for Leicester – a 2-1 home win against Ipswich in September 2000 – and scored ten in his first season, which a lot of top-flight strikers now wouldn't sniff at.

I felt sorry for him after the way he was portrayed. That famous celebration against Sunderland, when he took his shirt off and made men around the world feel like little boys, was him just letting it all out. But Ade was a cracking bloke: softly spoken, polite, and great with the youngsters. He'd help us wherever he could, and would sit next to us on the bikes when other first-teamers wouldn't. I really liked him.

I even got to experience Roberto Mancini at Leicester for a while. When he came, I was in the injury room a lot – he'd come in for a rub every morning, and though his English wasn't very good, we used to talk to each other a little bit. Who knows what he thought of being there at that time, though: he was only around for a month or so, before being offered the manager's job at Fiorentina.

Getting a bad knee injury in September 2000 definitely didn't do me any favours under Taylor, but the longer he stayed in charge, the less likely it seemed that I'd ever get a proper look-in at my local team. After their good start in his first season, though, results pretty much nosedived after Christmas: five wins from Boxing Day onwards after a 6-1 battering against Arsenal, including eight straight defeats towards the end of the season. And that was just in the league: no Leicester fan will forget that FA Cup quarter-final defeat to Wycombe in the same season.

When the 2001/02 campaign started with a 5-0 defeat to newly promoted Bolton Wanderers, it looked like he could be in trouble.

After I'd got fit again, I had been playing really well for the reserves, but it didn't seem to matter what I was doing. Garry Parker would say things to me like, 'You're the best I've seen at what you do', massively bigging me up.

'If I was first-team manager, I'd play you,' he told me. 'I don't know what the gaffer is thinking.'

Parks wasn't the same kind of player as me: he was very technical with great technique. He wasn't the quickest, but he could put the ball anywhere. Even in training as a coach he'd say, 'Watch this', before pinging a crossbar from 50 yards. Coaches tend to favour players who are like them, but you could tell he had a soft spot for me. He was a tongue-in-cheek joker with everyone – the banter king, even in bad times – but I thought he was fair to everyone and just genuinely thought I was good.

Not long after that, he had the chance to prove he wasn't bluffing.

On 1 October 2001 – one year to the day after Leicester had been top of English football – the club sacked Taylor as manager after a 2-0 defeat at The Valley. Parks was put in joint-charge with Tim Flowers, but before they could take charge of a game there was an international break: that unbelievable England game where David Beckham sent his country to the World Cup with a last-minute free-kick winner against Greece.

By that point, I'd started to drink a little bit on Friday nights. At the time, my games were Monday night football at Filbert Street or wherever else, but I wasn't getting anywhere near the first team – so it felt like it didn't matter. I wasn't regularly being stupid and getting hammered every weekend, but I hadn't really ever drank before that. My dad was a stickler for it and would massively discourage doing so when I was younger, so that always used to be in my head. But Friday night drinking became a thing for a while – and it almost cost me.

You know how people always say that you know who your friends are? Well, this was one of those moments. I was out with a few of the lads from City including a guy called James Miller, who had recently left the club as a youngster and was still playing at a good local standard. We were never massively close while at Leicester, but I always respected how hard he worked on the pitch and couldn't believe it when he didn't get offered a professional contract. I don't think he could, either.

On this night out, we'd come out of a club and there was a bit of commotion outside involving another group. There was a heavy police presence, and they were grabbing anyone who got a bit gobby … including me, who'd definitely had one too many on this occasion. In my drunken haze, I bumped into an officer who said something to me; thinking he was just another bloke, I told him where to go. He followed me a few steps, then tried to grab me – but the next thing I knew, Miller had come from nowhere and got in front of me, backing me against a supermarket window.

'If you're taking him, you're taking both of us – please don't worry officer, I'll take him home and put him to bed. He's just had a bit too much to drink.'

He really put himself at risk of getting arrested, but luckily there was a bit more commotion behind for the officer to deal with, so he left us alone.

The next day, I asked Miller why he'd done it.

'Because you don't need a police record in your career right now. You've actually got a chance of making it.'

From that day, he became one of my best friends – and still is now.

I think Parks had noticed this new behaviour in me, so he called me into his office one day and laid it all out.

'Listen, keep yourself fit – if you're going out at weekends, stop all of that. If Taylor gets sacked and I get the job, I'm putting you in.'

I was buzzing, but at the same time I thought, 'I bet you won't'. It's a big leap to go from nowhere near the first team, behind even some youth and reserve team players, not to mention those on the fringes of the senior squad. I got home and told my mum and dad, but knew I had to curb my excitement a bit because it probably wouldn't happen. Parks said he would bring me in, but when the pressure was on, would he actually?

As it turned out, the answer was yes. Straight away, I was training with the first team again – and eight days after Taylor's sacking, we had a game against Leeds in the League Cup at Filbert Street.

You're trying to work out where you stand in the gaffer's mind in training, when he says things like, 'You lot over there; you lot over with me.' I was counting, trying to see which group I'd been put in. Parks never gave anything away until the day of the game, though – that was just the way he liked to work. I knew I had a chance but thought I'd be on the bench, or maybe even in the extended squad. On the day of the match, I went into the training ground and saw the squad list: I was definitely in the 18, but didn't know anything more than that. The nerves start jangling. I rang my mum and dad from a toilet cubicle once again.

That day, I trained in the morning, went home to get a bit of sleep and watched my favourite 10 minutes of *The Shawshank Redemption* – I did that before every game I ever played in professional football. I'd take my DVD player with me anywhere I went and just watch that final sequence, where it talks about hope, because it put me in a good place to go and play.

But I left for the ground half an hour earlier than usual – if I was going to get a game that night, I wanted some new boots for it. I had a deal with Nike for kit at the time, but the ones I wanted wouldn't get there in time. I had my eye on a particular pair of Zooms, so I went to JJB Sports in town and bought some, brand new.

When you arrive at Filbert Street in your suit and tie – this time, wearing one that fits – you walk past your mates who are standing in the same position as you did when you weren't in the team; on the outside looking in. They were all there winking at me, slapping me on the back as I went into the ground. I sat down, then Parks came in and shut the door. Straight away, he whipped over the flipchart.

Right wing: Piper.

Finally, just after my 20th birthday, I was in. Parks dedicated part of his first team talk to me.

'This lad's deserved his chance – he's been smashing it in the reserves for me,' he said.

I was buzzing, and full of confidence. And then Leeds' squad came out: Martyn, Mills, Woodgate, Ferdinand, Harte, Bowyer, Bakke, Dacourt, Kewell, Keane, Viduka. *Jesus.*

I was nervous, but just had a really good feeling that night. Later in my career I'd get those same nerves in a different, much more debilitating way. This was pure excitement – finally, the chance to show what I could do.

I was already buzzing with the fact that I'd be playing against Ian Harte. Before the first whistle, I knew that it would be a running game for me, and that was the one I did best. I wanted to make him say 'fuck off' to me; I wanted to be relentless, to track every run he made.

But what I didn't factor in was just how good a player he actually was. The ball would get played out to him, I'd press him quickly to shut off his options, but he had this knack of being able to spin the ball around you down the line. I started angling my run to try to block that off, but then he'd just cut inside me quickly at the last second – then pass straight to someone like Mark Viduka. At the other end, you'd think you could shut him down for a cross and he'd still manage to squeeze it by you.

But I did well against him. He didn't know how to play me because I was new, and he gave me just enough space to enjoy myself out there. If he'd have cut off the line and put me on my left foot, I would have struggled massively running into traffic on the inside. The first few times he did it, I think he was offering me the challenge of trying to beat him. And I did. I got to the byline and whipped in a cross, which someone just headed over. From then, my confidence levels were flowing; Leicester fans were even shouting 'Pipinho' at me from the stands. I was buzzing every time I got the ball. Rio Ferdinand was coming out to double up on me – Jonathan Woodgate, too.

The only problem? We were 3-0 down at half-time. After 64 minutes, it was 6-0. Welcome to the first team. I remember creating a glorious chance for Sav towards the end, which he should have scored but fired straight at the keeper. We got absolutely battered, but from a completely selfish point of view I was buzzing. I'd waited a while for this.

The biggest thing I remember from that night is asking Ferdinand for his shirt midway through the second half, during a break in play. 'Course you can,' he told me. He got subbed with 20 minutes to go, though, and I remember thinking: *shit, we've got hammered and I'm not even going to get his shirt now*. But at the end of the game, I saw him standing in the tunnel with his shirt in his hands. Someone else had asked for it, but he'd said no – he was waiting for me. Not only that, he also asked for mine.

'Can I have yours? You're going to be a big player one day,' he told me.

I couldn't give him my debut shirt, though, so he got me to ask the kitman to send my other one out. But Macca – an absolute club legend who's been at Leicester since 1996, and not missed a first-team game since joining – was having none of it. So Rio never did get mine. It's probably not something he loses much sleep over these days.

Poor Parks was only in charge for that 6-0 cup defeat, but he'd stayed true to his word about putting me in the first team. I'll always be appreciative to him for that.

Leicester were bottom of the league after a miserable start, but it was time for change once more. Now, there was another new manager to impress – two of them, actually. Enter Dave Bassett and Micky Adams.

Little did I know, I'd be out as quickly as I'd got in.

CHAPTER 8

Stag, stag, stag, stag

'FORGET LAST night lads, it's all about the Premiership – we need to stay in it. Micky and I saw some things last night we liked, lots more than we didn't, but if we stick together as a group then we'll stay in this division.'

Dave Bassett said all of the right things in his first speech to Leicester players the morning after our battering from Leeds. For me, it was a new beginning after being out in the cold under Taylor – not least after my debut performance. After a bad opening to the season, it was a fresh start for everyone else as well.

I knew Bassett's reputation as an old-school former Wimbledon manager, but I got on really well with that kind of character – there was nothing hidden. If you were shit, he wouldn't mind letting you know that you were shit. If you were good, he would tell you. Right off the bat, I thought the players warmed to him. I liked his character, his cockney accent, and he seemed like the sort of manager we needed. Micky Adams, his No.2, would take charge of training, but at this point we didn't know that he was being groomed to become boss eventually.

All we knew of Micky was that he'd been a former pro himself, and had just come from being manager of Brighton. Funnily enough, it was Taylor who ended up replacing him there.

Dave and Micky's first game in charge was a trip to Chelsea at Stamford Bridge – and there was no way that I wasn't going to be in that team. If they'd seen what everyone else had done against Leeds, it was surely straightforward. I couldn't wait to play there.

But as usual, things weren't so straightforward in Leicester's 2001/02 season.

'Pipes, come see me in my office,' Bassett said.

So I did.

'We saw the game last night and you were our best player – speed, crossing ability, the lot.' Brilliant, gaffer – please tell me more.

'But ...'

There's always a 'but'.

'... we're in a dogfight right now, a scrap to stay in this league. We think you're a good player with a future at the club, but it would be beneficial for you to go out on loan. We're going with some older heads and experience to get us out of this.'

I travelled, but wasn't in the squad for Chelsea – not even on the bench. I was absolutely gutted. But I'd be lying if I said that I didn't like Bassett from the beginning – he just told me the truth. Even in short briefings, I respected the way that he and Micky operated.

In fairness, they did give me my Premiership debut against Liverpool seven days later. I already knew that I wouldn't be around for much longer at Leicester, but came on with 18 minutes to go at Filbert Street after replacing Matt Jones. Leicester were already 3-1 down and the game was basically gone, but I'll always remember how difficult an afternoon it was up front for Ade – I've never seen a striker so devoid of confidence in one match. He'd missed some big chances and the crowd were right on his back; so badly, in fact, that it genuinely made me wonder: do I really want to be a professional footballer?

At the other end, I watched Robbie Fowler finish off his hat-trick late on with a brilliant volley smashed past Ian Walker. I didn't get too many touches, though, and I remember looking at Liverpool, wondering how I was ever going to reach those standards. It was quicker than anything I'd ever seen before, and I'd already been in a team beaten 6-0. It definitely made me think that I wasn't effective as a substitute – I needed to start games.

Bassett had a couple of mates who managed lower-league teams and were looking for a winger like me. He wanted me to go and prove that I could perform consistently at a different level for a while, and thought it would toughen me up a bit. After that, he would bring me back. I was wounded at the time, but looking back I realise it was the best thing that could have happened for me then – no question. I think he and Micky both knew that, too: the chance to get games under my belt and gain more confidence somewhere else for a while.

It didn't take Bassett long to find me a club. Billy Dearden was Mansfield's boss, and they were flying high in the Third Division.

'Listen,' he said. 'My old mate Billy is keen to have you. I know you haven't got an agent, but I think it's the best thing for you. Go there, sign a three-month deal and we'll put a clause in there to bring you back at any time.'

Despite my initial disappointment, I was up for it. If that's what he thought would be good for me, I was up for having a go.

'Brilliant – they've got a game tonight. Meet them at Trowell Services. They're going to pick you up on the way. Good luck, work hard – I might need you with this lot.'

Sorry? Hours later, I was starting for Mansfield Town at Bristol Rovers.

At that point, it felt like I was leaving Leicester for good. I went into the training ground, stuffed my gear into a black bag and did the rounds to let my team-mates know what was going on. There wasn't time for much else – it was only a few hours later before I was sitting at that service station, absolutely bricking it. I couldn't help but think of the scene in *Forrest Gump*, where he gets on the bus and all of those kids are telling him that the seats are taken. That was about to be me.

Luckily, I couldn't have been more wrong – the Mansfield players were absolutely brilliant with me straight away. Dearden had a young side with ambition to go higher, and I found that out quickly. He was old-school like Bassett, only northern instead. I liked him straight away. 'How are you? You're going to be fucking dynamite here, son.'

He called someone from the back of the bus.

'Leroy! Make sure he's settled in, make sure he's sitting next to you – you boys stick together.'

'Leroy' was Lee Williamson: a central midfielder a little bit younger than me who went on to have a solid career with the likes of Watford, Sheffield United and Blackburn. Lee quickly became my best mate there, but they were all great lads.

Mansfield also had a few very experienced players in the team; veterans of hundreds of games like their goalkeeper Kevin Pilkington and left-winger Wayne Corden. They also had Liam Lawrence, who was my age and eventually got signed by Sunderland while I was at the club; Chris Greenacre, a striker who was banging in goals for fun; Bobby Hassell, who later spent a decade at Barnsley; and Craig Disley, another cracking player who was at Grimsby for years. They also had a player called Martin Pemberton, who looked just like me – we could have been brothers, I swear. It was a fantastic team that went on to get promoted – I was invited to their end-of-season party for being a part of it all, and went along.

Before that first game, I knew I'd love it – I felt at home straight away getting on that bus. No one was giving me a hard time. Well, not *too* much...

'We just hope you're better than that lad we signed on loan earlier in the season – he couldn't hit a fucking barn door, so we sent him back.'

'Haven't you played one game? You got hammered 6-0.'

Welcome aboard. I went straight into the starting XI and did really well on my debut, even after getting smashed by an early elbow in the face. I went down, but there was no sympathy.

'You're not in the fucking Premiership anymore,' my opponent said, helpfully.

The most amazing thing was that he knew who I was in the first place. I didn't score at Bristol Rovers, but we won 1-0 and everyone was cracking out cans for the way home. The coach dropped me back off at Trowell Services, where my mum was waiting to pick me up.

There was no cool-down; no getting in ice baths to recover for the next game. They were straight back on it. It was a culture shock, but a good one. The next day, when I turned up for training – getting changed at the stadium, obviously – everyone was buzzing to tell me what was in store.

'Hope you've brought your dogshit picker.'

And they weren't joking. Mansfield trained on a school pitch that was basically a public park. You'd arrive and there were cones turned over hiding little 'gifts' that we'd have to flick off the pitch. You know those wooden goals on school pitches where the crossbar was about two feet short? The goals were like that.

After training, there was no canteen – you'd go to the corner shop and get your own food. A lot of the players, these professional footballers, used to get corned beef cobs every day. I couldn't believe it at first, but soon grew to love the atmosphere there … no matter how much of a culture shock it was.

After training, I went back to the home team dressing room and folded up my kit in the middle.

'What are you doing? You take your kit home and wash it for tomorrow.'

Getting brought up at Leicester had been a different world. And how I was brought up at Leicester would be completely different to anything the club's young academy lads would experience today. There, you turned up at 10am with everything ready for you. At Mansfield, people shat in your shoes.

For some reason, we went on a mid-November break to Portugal for some warm-weather training – I think Billy was just up for the boozing. It was so much more relaxed: as long as you turned up for training the next day, it didn't matter what you did. So we'd be there sunbathing, daytime drinking, turning up to foam parties. It was crazy.

I roomed with Lee. We got back to our room one day and it absolutely stank. He knew exactly what it was – and who it was.

'Is the bathroom curtain closed?' he asked. 'Someone has shit in the bath.'

Sure enough, there it was – a Liam Lawrence special. Otherwise, it was a great tour.

In my second game for Mansfield, we were playing at our home ground of Field Mill against a York side featuring 26-year-old future Brighton manager, Graham Potter. We equalised to get a 1-1 draw in the last minute. In the next match, I scored my first professional league goal, against Swansea in a 3-0 win; Chris Greenacre had a shot which came back to me fast off the keeper and I just remember seeing the goal open up. I was desperate for it. In the youth team, I'd been used to scoring regularly playing as a striker – it was only towards the latter end of my development that they put me out wide.

I only ended up playing eight games for Mansfield, but picked up man-of-the-match awards in three-quarters of them. It felt like I could play at a higher level. I look back on that spell as one of my fondest times in football: I was injury free, and playing without any pressure at all.

Midway through my loan at Field Mill, I'd also been invited to Leicester's first-team Christmas party at a club called Undecided. It was fancy dress, so I went as a *Men In Black* agent. I'm not going to lie: I was bricking it … *again*. There was a (not-so) Secret Santa for first-team squad members, and we'd picked out names beforehand. There were two players I didn't want: Robbie Savage and Ian Marshall, because I'd have to batter one of them about something – you had to get up on stage to explain your choice – and I knew Robbie wouldn't like a young player doing that to him. Some of the others would have taken it with good humour I think, but I knew he wouldn't be like that.

I didn't want Marshall either, because although he could take a joke and was a hilarious bloke, he wouldn't let anything go. If I'd got him, he'd have pursued me for something until he'd got me back ten times worse. He didn't like anyone laughing at his expense.

So obviously, I pulled Sav out of the hat.

I went to some of the senior lads and asked them what I could get him without hammering him too much. Instead, they told me to do exactly that. They could see the turmoil that a young lad was going through … and naturally, they gave no shits. You just didn't do that sort of thing to first-team guys, though, especially one who I knew wouldn't like a joke going against him.

But I didn't have much choice. Muzzy said to me, 'Every morning he comes in and his breath stinks – the lads cane him for it all the time.' I didn't know that, but I went with it anyway. Matt Elliott suggested I buy him a massive gas mask, but Muzzy's idea was a bit simpler – a massive tub of mints. When it was my turn, I got up on stage.

'I've got this guy this gift, because I've heard that his breath fucking *stinks* in the morning.'

Out came the mints from my Christmas bag, to cheers from everyone in the room.

'Can Robbie Savage please come up to accept his present?'

Everybody was laughing, but Sav didn't look happy. He pulled the mic off me, mock laughed into it and then slung the mints behind him. Never mind.

Stefan Oakes did a little speech when it was his turn.

'I know he's come in with a big price tag, but I think he needs a little more help – so I've got him this book.'

It was for kids: *How to Play Football and Improve.*

'Ade, if you'd like to come to the stage, please …'

Ade took it really well to be fair, and was laughing along with everyone else. Oakesey continued: 'If you'd like to turn to page five, it's all about first touch.' It went down well.

Dennis Wise had only signed for Leicester that summer, so wasn't really involved in the Secret Santa, but it didn't stop him getting a gift for someone and getting up on stage.

'I know I've not been here for long lads, but I thought it would be rude of me not to buy someone a present.

I've got you this mate, because you're the only prick in a Leicester shirt.'

Dennis pulled out a vibrator decorated with a little blond wig and mini Leicester kit on.

'Sav, come and get your gift.'

Those two *hated* each other. Just like he did with me, Robbie walked up on stage, pretended to have a laugh about it and then threw the dildo away with my mints. I didn't feel so bad after that – in hindsight, he was probably alright about mine. But with Dennis? He was fuming. And then he disappeared.

That was the last present of the night, so everyone dispersed into their own groups and cracked on. As Frank Sinclair was teaching us a drinking game with playing cards, the mic came on again. It was Sav, with his back to everyone. Then he turned around.

'Hi everyone, my name's Dennis and I've just come out of a meeting with the gaffer.'

To make his point, he'd rubbed chocolate fudge cake on the end of his nose, trying to indicate that Wisey was a brown-noser. The room stayed silent.

Back at Mansfield, I wasn't allowed to play for them in the FA Cup, so missed their 4-0 win over Second Division Huddersfield in the second round. And I definitely couldn't play for them in the third: at Filbert Street, against Leicester. I thought my dad was taking the piss when he told me what the draw was, and my phone was like a hotline straight afterwards. It was a bit weird sitting up in the stands for it, and I remember thinking how much I wished that I was playing for Mansfield that afternoon. It could have been a chance to show Leicester that I was better than some of the current squad, and make them question why they had me out on loan.

In January 2002, Billy Dearden left to join Notts County as their new manager. Mansfield's No.2 was a guy called Stuart Watkiss, who took over for the rest of the season. He was a good coach. He didn't know whether he'd be in charge for the following season, but was trying to make some plans in case he was. And he wanted to know how I would feel if he put an offer in to buy me from Leicester? They thought £250,000 might do it.

I said yes – because I did love it there. I was playing every week, they were going to put me on more money and things were going well. It sounds stupid now really, because I had a chance of making it at Leicester – and in truth, I think half of me knew that I wouldn't go to Mansfield permanently. I didn't think Leicester would say yes anyway, but if they did, I would know they didn't really want me properly. It was almost a win-win for me. So Stuart had a go. But not only did Leicester say no, they also told him that they wanted to recall me. The first-team situation still wasn't great – four games without a league win while I was away – and they'd heard things were going particularly well for me at Mansfield.

I remember putting a bit of an act on for them, telling Stuart that I couldn't believe I was going back so soon, that I probably won't get in the team anyway. But inside, I was thinking the opposite: if I was heading back to Filbert Street, then I'd be playing.

Surely?

CHAPTER 9

Down with the Leicester

AS A young player, I preferred going into an environment where the team was struggling – I had nothing to lose.

People were expecting performances from the experienced pros and players who'd cost money – not me. If I didn't have a great game, no one was going to look at me; not while everyone else around me was suffering. So when I returned to Leicester, it felt like I had the freedom to just go out there and play. It felt good straight away.

Spirits in the dressing room were still high – despite how crap everything was going results-wise, the lads were still joking around with each other. They were gutted to be losing, don't get me wrong, but it didn't really change the dynamics of what went on behind the scenes. Matchdays were hard because the team was losing and fans were on their backs – and even from a cynical perspective, some players might have been worried about losing wages because of clauses in their contracts. But it didn't feel like doom and gloom at Filbert Street. The local media weren't really battering us, and somehow it just felt like a comfortable environment to play in.

My first game back was at West Brom in the FA Cup. I came on for the last 10 minutes, after they'd just scored a penalty. We lost 1-0. But I remember feeling sharp. The team was struggling, and I could see myself playing in it – I had that belief within me.

My second Premiership game for Leicester was against the same opposition as my first: Liverpool, only this time at Anfield for a daunting Wednesday night trip. I'd had a good week's training, but didn't know I was starting until Bassett told us our line-up at the hotel pre-match. I was playing up front, too, alongside James Scowcroft.

I didn't know who the Liverpool player Steven Wright was at the time – although I'd later end up joining Sunderland less than a week after him. But I knew Jamie Carragher, and I thought that although he was a brilliant defender, there was a chance to get in behind him. I was quicker than him, and also Sami Hyypia and Stephane Henchoz. I didn't love playing up front, but thought I might be able to work off Scowcroft, who was really supportive and great in the air – just like Brian Deane was at that time. If the ball went long, I knew one of those two would win it, so it'd be my job to guess where they were going to plant it. I got a lot of balls working off Deano like that in the Premiership.

And who was at the other end? Emile. I remember looking down the other end of the pitch thinking how I had been cleaning his boots two years ago. Everything had moved on so much. Growing up at Leicester, I'd always looked up to him as *the* man. I remember him most from my days as a ball boy; he'd have been 16 or so and playing for the youth team. Len Mawby would report back on their matches when we saw him afterwards, and every single week we'd ask for the score and who got our goals. It was always similar: 'Won 4-0, Emile scored all four' or, 'Won 3-1, Emile got two of them.' The guy sounded like a legend even then, and he was only a youth player. Later, I was doing well at that level and people were talking about me in similar ways, but I was cleaning Emile's boots when he was at the next level, banging in goals for the first team.

Emile was a better player than I was, no doubt – even with my injuries, he was huge as a favourite son of Leicester. But looking down that pitch to him was an important moment, because I'd always been behind him; now we were sharing the same pitch on opposite sides. Liverpool beat us 1-0 at Anfield that night – and guess who scored the winner?

They were brilliant; it was so sharp. Playing in games like that takes you back to that first time you were involved with the youth team at 14 – but really, any time you take a step up. Then the question is: can you handle it? I know we lost, and players don't tend to care about individual displays after that, but as a young lad I remember coming off that pitch and feeling pleased with myself. You're gutted to lose, but when you're breaking in, you need to do well for yourself.

Match-winner Emile gave me his shirt afterwards, but not at the ground – he came round to my house, as I used to live near someone else he knew. It was like being a youth team player all over again. He got the shirt out of his boot, signed it for me and then sat in my living room having a cup of tea.

That Liverpool game had given me good grounding, because I'd done well against some top players. I didn't get the ball much, but had a couple of half-opportunities and had given Steven Wright some problems drifting over to the left. Against Chelsea in our next game, Gianfranco Zola was the best player on the pitch – and I know this will sound so big-headed, but I honestly think it was me after that. I was a Marcel Desailly fanboy before the game, but he brought me down for a stonewall penalty that didn't get given and I gave him a horrible time. I was up top with Scowcroft again, who was dominant in the air and scored both of our goals from corners. I was often just running beyond him. It regularly came down to a straight race between Desailly and me, and he was ageing. I should have scored in that game, but Carlo Cudicini made an unbelievable save.

There were certain players who weren't having a great time of things at all, which did make it easier for me at the time. A lot of Peter Taylor's signings were very good at what they did in training, but I didn't see those kinds of players as legends. You imagine a kid at a huge club now, getting into a team littered with ridiculous players – that imposter syndrome would be off the charts. The lack of that helped my own transition into the team for sure.

I was starting every game by this point – but Leicester were still losing; five on the bounce from that Liverpool game. The worst was getting picked apart 3-0 at home to Derby. On the Tuesday morning after that game, I got my first bit of criticism since I had broken into the first team. I was getting quite a lot of letters from fans at that time, and I opened one that I thought was going to be along similar lines, telling me how well I was doing. It was from an older fan, who started his letter with, 'I've really enjoyed your performances for Leicester this season ...'

Go on.

'... but I've got to say, there's no point playing well against the Chelseas of this world if you're going to be absolutely shocking against Derby. You were awful.'

If I read that sort of thing now, it wouldn't touch me. But back then? It killed me. I drove home without talking to anyone; this guy had caned me, explaining everything I wasn't good at. But I kept it to remind myself that you're only ever one game away from getting hammered.

Daft things were happening to the team. We went to Middlesbrough and lost 1-0, with Frank Sinclair bobbling the only goal beyond his own goalkeeper from 40 yards. A 1-1 draw against Charlton stopped the rot of defeats, and I assisted Scowy for the opening goal of the game – probably the first time in my life that I'd crossed a ball with my left foot and it reached its destination. I celebrated like it was my goal, stood in front of the Kop with my arms outstretched. To have that feeling for the first time was unbelievable – I wanted more of it.

We were sinking without a trace into the First Division, though – 12 points adrift of safety with nine games to go. I honestly don't think the players' drive had gone, though. I looked around that dressing room and there was genuine passion to do well. Muzzy was a born winner – he hated losing every week. You'd play with him while looking up to him, thinking he was as good as Paul Scholes. It was a rose-tinted view, no doubt, but ability-wise he was unbelievable; when I was breaking through, he was on a pedestal in the eyes of the younger lads.

Another draw at Southampton didn't help us out much, but I was playing well on a personal level: I assisted Brian Deane for one of his two goals. That game was also significant because Gordon Strachan later told me that it was the one which had convinced him to try to sign me that summer.

Because he trusted in his squad, he often targeted players who'd done well against them – particularly Wayne Bridge, who he really rated and had played at left-back. Apparently,

Bridge told Strachan I'd given him his toughest challenge of the season.

Leicester's financial situation must have been dodgy then, because players were flying out the exit. Ade had left for Crystal Palace on a permanent deal by February 2002, while Tim Flowers, Simon Royce, Junior Lewis, Arnar Gunnlaugsson, Jacob Laursen and Damien Delaney were all sent out on loan. Trev was sent to three different clubs in less than four months. A lot of Leicester's young lads were getting into the team around this part of the season: my mate Jon Stevenson had made his debut against West Ham in January while I was out on loan at Mansfield, and managed to get his nose broken six minutes after coming on. But while the club were heading towards administration, they also believed they had a good crop of young lads who'd come through the youth system together. Matt Heath, Jordan Stewart, Jon Ashton, Martin Reeves, Stevo – I'd played with them all. I knew we had a strong youth team, because Jon Rudkin moved through the age groups with us rather than staying at the same level. He didn't want to leave us.

After my eighth Premiership game, I was still waiting for a win in Leicester colours. In March, we played Leeds at home again – only a 2-0 defeat this time, with Fowler scoring against us once more, having signed from Liverpool only a month after his hat-trick against us. Finally, we beat Blackburn 2-1 at Filbert Street, and Mark Hughes – who'd made his league debut for Manchester United before I was even born – scored Rovers' goal in his last season of professional football.

Everybody knew relegation was waiting around the corner to put us out of our misery, but when it finally came in a home match against Manchester United, it didn't feel like we were going down for the first time in seven years. Ole Gunnar Solskjaer scored the only goal in a 1-0 defeat, but we actually gave United a good match. Ryan Giggs even came up to me at the end and congratulated me.

I'm not just saying this to curry favour from Leicester fans, but they were absolutely unbelievable that afternoon – they sang all game. We were going down after a shocking season, but it was like a party at Filbert Street. They didn't go quiet on their team, and they didn't stop. Once again, the pressure from that situation was just lifted, and because of that I think the players responded positively.

Micky Adams took over as manager full-time after that – he was supposed to get the job at the end of the season, but it made sense for him to take the reins at that point. Bassett went upstairs to become director of football. I liked Dave a lot because he'd been upfront with me from the start, then put me in the team and kept me there. He would have one-on-ones with me in the office that I really appreciated.

But I also really liked Micky. He'd been a very good No.2 because he had good banter and was well liked by the players. When he took over with all of these youngsters in the side, it must have been an exciting time for him, too. I know we got relegated, but there were some good prospects to get behind. Micky himself was a good young manager with a lot of ideas and the personality to go with it.

His first game was against Everton at Goodison Park. We blew a two-goal lead in that game, after Deano had scored twice in the first half – again – but I remember we played well. And the one thing I remember from it? Putting one on a plate for my old mate Stefan Oakes, who blazed over the bar from six yards out. I hope he reads this and remembers it.

When Bassett moved upstairs, it gave Micky the freedom to be who he wanted to be. Before, he couldn't really do that because he wasn't the gaffer. He was a fun manager to play for, who trusted in your ability to go out there and perform for him – there weren't too many constraints on me, for example, which I really liked.

But he ran the bollocks off everybody. Micky wanted a fit side. When I was coming through the youth team, if the coaches wanted you to run they'd say, 'Right, we're going to Bradgate Park' – a really big country park just outside of Leicester. Micky was the first manager I played under who introduced disguised running – where you'd have a ball at your feet, but you'd also be grinding your own balls off in the process.

I tried to take it up another level, though. I didn't feel like I was finishing matches strongly; I was knackered on 70 minutes – you could have touched me and I'd have fallen over. So I asked the physios to come up with this regime for me to improve: something called four on, three off, where you'd run flat out for the first four minutes, then drop it down for three – four times. I was doing it the day before our next game against Aston Villa, famous for the most expensive dump of Robbie Savage's life in Graham Poll's toilet and George Boateng chucking one of Paul Dickov's boots into the East Stand. But Micky walked in on me.

'What the bloody hell are you doing?! You don't run like this the day before a match – what's the matter with you?'

And then he educated me. You get fit Monday, Tuesday, Wednesday; a little bit on Thursday; never a Friday. He hammered me, but I deserved it. I just wanted to be the fittest out of the whole squad and last the full distance in matches.

Micky goes down as one of the top three managers I played under, along with Peter Reid and Mick McCarthy. They all had a similar approach with me: just go and play. They were straight with me and didn't beat around the bush. I'm not good with condescending personalities who talk down to you; those who leave you in the dark wondering what point they were trying to get across. I had that later in my career.

Against Villa, I was up against Steve Staunton – by then 33 years old after a great career. We had a corner, and he collared me.

'Oi, you little fucker.'

'What's up, Steve?'

'You ought to slow down or stay away from me lad, or else I'll take you out.'

I just laughed at him. 'Old man can't keep up?'

'Exactly. So stay the fuck away from me.'

I loved stuff like that – he was letting me know I was doing well.

I was still on my £375-per-week contract that Taylor had put me on. We drew 0-0 at Fulham in our penultimate game of the season, and there was a two-week break for the FA Cup Final before our last match at Filbert Street against Tottenham. Finally, the club told me that they were ready to open negotiations for a proper new contract. I was buzzing.

Just before Dean Sturridge had left for Wolverhampton Wanderers in November 2001, he'd played in my debut match against Leeds. Not long after that, he had asked me if I had an agent. I didn't.

'Well who looks after you?'

'I don't know … my dad.'

'You need to talk to my brother.'

Dean's brother was Simon, the father of Daniel Sturridge. I didn't sign with him at the time, but we said we'd talk when the time came. Eventually, it did – Bassett asked me if I had an agent, so I gave him Simon's name.

'Tell him I want to meet him next week.'

I'd met Simon before but didn't really know him. So there we were, sitting in the canteen, waiting for Bassett to call us in. I didn't want to go in – I just wanted Simon to take care of everything.

'Don't worry, he'll be cool – just come in.'

So I did – and I sat there, staying as quiet as a mouse.

'Right, let's not drag it out – how much do you want?'

'Well, we were looking for £5,000 a week,' Simon said. Bassett was livid.

'FIVE GRAND A WEEK?! Are you fucking mad? I've got Paul Dickov out there, a Scotland international, and he's not even on that. Pipes, are you understanding this?'

I didn't want to ask for that – I thought it was too much. This was going wrong quickly. But I didn't want to speak up, so Simon tried to calm him down. And then it went very wrong.

'Get out.'

Well that has gone fucking brilliantly.

'Not you Pipes, him – he's getting out.'

So Simon did, leaving me in the room to face the music. I didn't want to do a contract negotiation there and then, for the risk of Bassett having me on toast.

'Listen mate,' he said. 'You aren't getting five grand a week. What do you think is fair? Because I'll tell you what

I think is. I've met your old man a few times before, and he seems like a reasonable bloke – bring him here now and we'll get this sorted.'

Simon told me it was a massive mistake to do that, explaining that my dad would get bullied. But he clearly hadn't met my old man. And he'd just been chucked out of the office. So I rang my dad at work. 'I'll be there in 10 minutes,' he said.

Simon had stuck around just in case he was needed, but my dad stopped him in his tracks. 'I'll sort this out – I'm not having this.'

This whole episode encapsulates my dad to a tee. We went in, and before Bassett could even get his pleasantries in, there was a slap on the table.

'No, no, no. Before I sit down, you see this young boy here?'

Please don't …

'He's been at this football club since he was eight years old.' Bassett opened his mouth again, but there was no point. 'Let me finish, Mr Bassett. Eight years old! He's not asked for as much as a fucking chocolate biscuit so far. All I'm telling you to do is give my son what's right.'

I think Bassett liked it, but he had a comeback.

'He's not worth five grand a week yet, Mr Piper. It's alright doing all of these skills on the wing, but he's not even scored a Premiership goal yet. Don't get me wrong, he's been brilliant so far – but if he isn't scori…'

'I'll tell you now, Mr Bassett – before the end of the season, he'll score a goal for Leicester. Give him three grand a week.'

'I'll give him £2,500.'

'You alright with that, son? Good. Deal.'

Simon was hammering my dad in the car park, but the comeback was easy: 'You got thrown out of the office with nothing, mate. You're not his agent any more – I am.'

So there we were: a minor victory in a car park and down to the last ever game at Filbert Street, before the move to the new Walkers Stadium [later the King Power Stadium]. Wouldn't that be a nice occasion to finally score for Leicester City?

CHAPTER 10

The last goal

I HONESTLY can't remember what the build-up to the Tottenham game was like, but people were wondering who would score the last goal at Filbert Street. I certainly wasn't thinking about it.

Before the game, I'd been presented with Leicester's Young and Most Improved Player of the Year awards, and as I was driving up to the ground, I could see loads of 'Piper 29' shirts. It was an unbelievable feeling – I can't even imagine what that's like for the massive players of today.

Up to that match, I'd played 16 games for my hometown club. We'd won one of them. But having played well since I came back from Mansfield, and with Micky Adams as manager, there were plenty of reasons to be optimistic about the future.

But first, we had to wave goodbye to Filbert Street – opened way back in 1891, and the home of many special memories for me. That was the case even before what happened against Tottenham on 11 May 2002.

In that game, I felt like I was floating – everything I tried just seemed to come off. Stepovers, nutmegs, giving Ben Thatcher and Anthony Gardner the absolute runaround. I had my shirt untucked, felt like there was no pressure and didn't care – I just felt that confident.

But Tottenham scored first. It had been goalless at half-time, but then Teddy Sheringham tucked away a penalty nine minutes after the break. Luckily, their lead didn't last long: six minutes later, we were level through Paul Dickov.

I knew where my mum, dad and brother were sitting, because I'd sorted them the tickets. I also had a lot of friends in the ground that day. But despite the history at stake, despite the feeling that this game was going brilliantly on a personal level, I never imagined that I'd score in it. I wasn't even bothered about it, to be honest – I was just living in the moment. That's when I played my best football.

I'd only ever scored one header in my life – in that school game in Liverpool, against Kevin Nolan's team. I just couldn't head a ball; it was like the Hunchback of Notre Dame getting up there. But in the 71st minute against Spurs, it happened.

When Alan Rogers launched in a throw-in from the left, I was standing at the back post, watching the flight of the ball and thinking it had nothing to do with me. We hadn't specifically worked on attacking the box from a long throw – it was just one of those things. I was standing there next to Thatcher, this beast with a massive head and massive thighs, and saw Matt Elliott going up to flick the ball on. *Shit, if he wins this I might have a chance here ...*

He got up and won the ball. There were a million things going through my head in two seconds at this point – and I'm not just making this up to make the story sound better. It's your mum in the back garden training you up as a toddler; it's running around as a little kid and your dad telling you that you aren't good enough; it's him explaining why I didn't have the heart to play at this level; it's Dave Bassett telling you that you haven't even scored a Premiership goal yet.

The last thought was a bit simpler: *I am heading this ball.* Thatcher tried to swing a boot and clear it away, but because I wanted that goal so badly, I caught it sweetly. I hit the deck, but Kasey Keller was going the other way and I knew it was going in. It felt like the world had gone into slow-motion. I saw the ball fly past Callum Davidson and over Stevo's head, then ripple the net.

I wish I had jumped in the Kop afterwards – I still think about that now. I just pointed at them instead ... or more specifically, to my dad. I wanted to let him know that he had said I couldn't do this. More than half of me making it as a footballer was to prove him wrong, I think. It might have been parental psychology all along and he was just an absolute mastermind, but I'll never know for sure.

Scoring that goal made me feel like I'd arrived: not making my debut, or the good performances building up to it. That goal.

My boots from that game are in the reception area at the King Power Stadium now – I donated them to the club. I had two shirts from that game: you played in one, and had another spare. Post-match, all of those kits were collected up by the kitman and auctioned off for charity. But I had to keep that one – how could I not? So in the end, my second shirt got auctioned off. I'm very sorry to whoever won it. The real one is hanging up in my home gym, signed by the full squad.

I finally put pen to paper on my new contract the following week. We were going down, but things felt good: the crowd liked me, I liked the manager and we were in for a new season. We'd be back.

Or at least most of us would.

Throughout the summer, the club were ringing me to say that the replica shirt they'd sold most of had 'Piper 29' on the back. By then, it looked like Muzzy had played his last game for the club, and a few other players left that summer: Gary Rowett went to Charlton, Sav headed for Birmingham, while Lee Marshall also left for West Brom. The club were putting me on their promotional posters for the 2002/03 season and I was loving life. It felt like they were trying to build the team around me.

We headed to Finland on pre-season – Micky Adams' first trip with us as a manager. He was great for things like that: we were there to be professional and work hard, and he had a lot of staff around him to look after us. But if we did all of that, we could go out a couple of times – he trusted us as players to go and do that, so long as nobody was getting slaughtered.

We actually didn't even go out that much in Finland – I remember one really good night there, but otherwise, players would just nip down to the hotel bar when they fancied it. Every night there was a card school that the older pros played in – not for huge money, like I've heard with Michael Owen dropping £30,000 at the 2002 World Cup; a few hundred quid, maybe. We had a lot of younger lads like myself on that tour, and often we'd just sit in the room and watch the others playing – otherwise, it could be quite boring if you weren't going out.

One night, we were in there when Callum Davidson accused Dennis Wise of cheating. Wise had won a hand, but there was a stray card near him and Davidson had called him out for it. 'Fuck off am I cheating. I'd never do that,' Dennis hit back.

It was back and forth, but nothing violent. Eventually, it got to the point where they decided to just stop playing, and everyone dispersed quite quickly. A few grumbles afterwards maybe, but nothing you'd be too concerned about. Move along, nothing to see here.

Wise was in the room next to Jordan Stewart and me; Callum was in with Paul Dickov, and called it a night. He took off his glasses and hit the sack, but Dickov said he was going down to the bar with a few of the other lads for a bit. Paul left the door on the latch, so it was ajar. The rest of us – including Dennis – also went to bed.

The next thing we knew, there was shouting and screaming in the hallway. It was carnage. I opened my door to look out and check what the hell was going on. Wise was standing nearest to me with his back to our door, and Matt Elliott was holding back Gerry Taggart. But both of them were going absolutely nuts at him, calling him every name you could think of.

'You've always been the fucking same, Wisey.'

Dennis was backing up as he was talking back, but they went for him. He shot into his room to the sound of locks and chains.

'That little bastard has gone into Callum's room and knocked him out while he's asleep.'

You *what?*

Taggs was banging on Wise's door telling him to open up, but it wasn't happening. It turned out that Dennis had knocked on Callum's door and got no answer, but as it was ajar, he had just gone in anyway. He woke him up. By this point, Cal was just confused – not least as Dennis was only there to apologise. Or so it seemed.

'I can't believe all of that kicked off – just came to say sorry,' he said.

'No worries mate, it's all good.'

Callum went to offer him his hand, but Wise grabbed it and pulled him on to a haymaker. *Smack*, he dropped him on to his bed. And then he hit Callum twice more, fracturing his cheekbone. That's when all of the commotion kicked off.

The next morning at breakfast, Callum was downstairs in a state, having been to hospital to get himself looked at. Micky addressed him.

'Cal, I know it's a nightmare mate, but Dennis wants to come down and say something.'

He did, but nobody was looking at him.

'Listen, lads …'

'No, fuck off – nobody wants to hear what you've got to say,' someone told him.

'I just wanted to apologise.'

'Fuck off, Wisey.'

He shrugged his shoulders and walked off. Micky went with him, then came back.

'I've sent him home – he's on the next flight. Can't have that in my team.'

The worst part was that I actually liked Dennis – he was really good with the young lads, and very supportive. But I loved Callum Davidson, so my allegiances would always lie with him. He was a great lad, and one of the nicest pros you could ever meet. Dennis just couldn't handle being called a cheat.

Otherwise, that Finland trip was great, and helped us to prepare for our first game in the new Walkers Stadium against Athletic Bilbao. For a long time, it looked like we were going to lose it: despite them having ten men from the 28th minute (who gets sent off in pre-season?), they'd scored in the second half and led 1-0 going into stoppage time. But then Jordan Stewart scored a header. Being a winger, if you create a goal for someone, you want them to run to you first. When he didn't, I thought, 'You cheeky little bastard.' Me and Jordan were best mates – all of the young lads were really close – but he binned me off. At that point, I think the 'Piper 29' shirt sales had massaged my ego a bit. I should have been buzzing that my mate had scored, not worrying that he didn't run to me.

Micky couldn't sign many players that summer, but he was able to bring in Billy McKinlay and Nicky Summerbee – initially without even paying them while the club was hurtling towards administration. I'd watched Nicky Summerbee for years when I was growing up, thinking he was a top player: his passing, his crossing, his vision. Looking at that team, I thought it was going to be an unbelievable season – Muzzy was staying after all, and Micky still had a great core of players who could help the club get back up to the top flight.

But I wasn't going to be one of them.

It got to the first game of the season against Watford and I'd been ill the night before. Elliott had been too, but Micky thought he could handle it. I could go home and put my feet up, he said – there were bigger and better things coming for me on Monday morning. I thought I'd been called up for England Under-21s – I was buzzing. Monday morning came, and I got in early. There was a message on reception for me to go and see the manager.

When I got there, Micky said Leicester had received an offer for me from Sunderland of £2.5m, rising to £3.5m.

'… and the club have accepted it.'

I was in there on my own and just said outright, 'I don't want to go.'

Micky and Dave didn't put too much pressure on me at that point, but told me to go and speak with the Sunderland manager Peter Reid – that he was a good bloke. Reid had sent people down for the last few months of the season to watch me, and had told Leicester that he liked what he'd seen, wanted to start me and would also hand over the No.7 shirt. I would have been one of their big signings for the start of the Premiership season.

I got out of the room and rang my dad. 'The club have sold me to Sunderland.'

He was actually really supportive of the move, telling me it was a brilliant opportunity that I shouldn't say no to. We got in the car to go up there the following day – little did I know, it took three and a half hours to do so – so there was a lot of talking time on that journey. He explained that I needed to be happy, but with the way he was going about the conversation, you could tell he wanted me to sign up there and stay in the Premiership. On the way up, we got a call from Reid.

'Listen, don't come all the way up to Sunderland on an evening – come and meet me in this pub in Yarm.'

I liked Reid from that very first call – it was relaxed, and made me feel at ease. Mark Blackbourne, the director of football operations, was there with him when we arrived. You could tell that they both liked my dad. When the subject turned to football, Peter said, 'Listen, we like you. We've watched you for months. We're going to put you straight in, you'll be the ammunition for Kevin Phillips and Niall Quinn. You love to get down the line and put crosses in, and that's what we need. We want you, and we're willing to offer you a good contract.'

He looked at Blackbourne, who clearly hadn't been briefed about doing negotiations there and then. 'Just give him an idea of what he could get, Mark.'

So Blackbourne asked for a pen from the bar, got a napkin and wrote down a five-year contract with a sum of money next to each one. It started at £5,000 per week for the first year, and went up in £1,000 increments for every year after that. On top of that, I'd get a £250,000 signing-on fee, paid in £50,000 instalments at the start of every season, plus a £2,500 appearance fee. It would have doubled my current Leicester deal and then some. My dad looked at it and made a face, then passed it to me. In that moment, I thought it made me a millionaire. Obviously I was happy with it.

'No, no, no – we're not happy with that,' my old man said. 'We're going to need a bit more than that, but we can talk about it down the line because he's still undecided.'

We said our goodbyes, and I told Peter I was honoured that he wanted me to play for Sunderland. But I also told him that I didn't want to leave Leicester. That was my parting remark.

'Look, mate – Leicester are in the shit … they need the money. There's no way they aren't selling you this summer. I'll ring you tomorrow and we'll see where you're at, but I think you need to be a Sunderland player sooner rather than later from what I've been told.'

Next, as I remember it, I was confronted by a furious Micky Adams wondering why I'd turned them down. We went into his office.

'Why would you tell them no? Why wouldn't you want to display your skills at that level?'

At that point, I got the feeling he didn't think I was ambitious enough to make that move. But it was just because I genuinely wanted to stay at Leicester.

'Well you're not training, because if you get injured, we definitely can't sell you. We're on the brink of administration and need the money.'

I had it in my head that I was going to wait it out and stand firm until things calmed down a bit. Sunderland's season was about to start and they would need to target someone else if I kept digging my heels in.

I came in the next morning and Micky had the same stance: 'You're not training with us today – go and do some work in the gym.' Later, someone came to get me and I was back in his office.

'This is how desperate the club needs you gone, Pipes,' he says. 'They've accepted a £2.5m offer from Southampton for you. Get your dad and go to see Gordon Strachan this afternoon.'

'Gaffer, how many times have I got to tell you? I don't want to leave.'

'Go and see Gordon Strachan.'

So we got in the car again and headed for St Mary's. I liked Strachan, just not quite as much as Reid. He told me the story of what Wayne Bridge had said about me, and I was pretty chuffed about it. Rupert Lowe, the chairman, came in and reiterated what Strachan had said – they really wanted me, and someone would show me around the city to look at places I might want to buy a house. The club would look after me.

'I know you've got a decision to make between us and Sunderland,' said Strachan, 'and I'll be honest: we can't match what they could pay you. But are you about the money or where you're going to develop best as a player?'

I liked both managers, to be fair – they were honest, but Reid had a bit more banter and I felt like I'd be more comfortable under him. But I went back in the next day and told Leicester that I didn't want to play for either of them – I was staying put.

And that's when the mood turned. Me trying to stand strong stopped being cute. The local lad who wanted to stick around and help his hometown team get back in the top flight wasn't going to wash. Over the next few days, I did take part in a session – but it was just shooting practice with the reserves. I smashed one over the crossbar.

'Jesus, £3.5m? You'd better take it while you can, mate.'

It was Micky. I didn't mind it to be honest, but then in a quieter moment it got a bit too personal.

'Think of all those people who've been here as long as you who'll lose their jobs if you don't leave.'

I don't blame Micky in the slightest – if it had been up to him, I'd have stayed at Leicester. Knowing the inner workings of a football club like I do now, the hierarchy were probably on to him daily putting the pressure on, telling him to get in my ear and stressing that if I didn't go, a dire situation was just around the corner. The timing just wasn't right. Muzzy and I were probably the biggest saleable assets that the club had that summer, but nobody came in for him after he'd signed his new contract, and in the end he was a massive part of why Leicester went straight back up. I was the only one they could get that kind of money for.

Ade Akinbiyi had left Leicester by then, but I was chatting to him about my situation. He asked me who my agent was, and explained that this was a big deal for me.

'You can't have your dad do a deal like that, mate – not in the Premiership.'

So he put me in touch with his representative Andrew Mills, and my dad was actually really supportive about it. He knew that Ade had got some brilliant moves in his career, and suggested I give him a call.

I liked Andrew immediately. He came across as a bit of a wide boy on the phone but could back it up with some of the players he had at the time. He had a history of sorting out big moves for his players. I told him I wanted to stay at Leicester, but that I still wanted him to look after me and we'd see what happened.

'No, no – you've got to move. There's no way you can stay with an opportunity like this.'

He wasn't the only one who thought that. I spoke with Brian Deane, whose advice was straightforward: it's a short career and this was a great opportunity to stay in the Premiership while tripling my current wages. The club needed me gone.

Deano was like my footballing dad – he'd give me great advice on all sorts of things, often staying behind to work with me. Instead of going into town after training, spending our money on clothes – or the amusements, as I liked to – he'd say, 'No, we'll go for a nice meal and a chat instead. Come on.'

We'd go to San Carlo on Granby Street, sit down and I'd just listen to him. 'Don't always wear your trackies, don't always wear your caps and ripped jeans – put on some trousers and a nice shirt; represent yourself well.' He still does it now. He's never been out of touch with me since those Leicester days. When things were going wrong and I was lost to addiction, he'd be on the phone offering his support; offering to come down from Yorkshire for a game of golf. He'd give me advice on looking after money, keeping the right company, looking after myself. He's an unbelievable bloke. I was brought up really well by my mum and dad, but he could pass on his own experiences having come from a similar background to me. I try to pass on some of the stuff that Deano taught me to some of the kids I coach now.

When it came to leaving Leicester, I remember Muzzy and Elliott telling me to just go if they offered £10,000 per week; that I should be playing Premiership football because I'd proved I could play at that level. Because the club was in such a financial mess, we didn't even know if Leicester could get back there or not.

Fuck it, I thought. I'm going – and I'm choosing Sunderland. So what now, then?

'I'll fly up there,' said my new agent Mills. 'You drive up with your dad and come pick me up from the airport. Tell me what you want, and I'll go in and get it for you.'

Mills walked out of Newcastle Airport with a gelled mohican, light grey suit with pink pinstripes, and pink crocodile skin shoes to match. In his hand was a Louis

Vuitton briefcase. These were well before the days of whacking his name into Google or social media to see what he looked like, so you can imagine what was going through our heads.

'I know what you're thinking,' he started, 'but this is just my flamboyant side coming out in the way I dress. I will get you what you want.'

We sat outside the Stadium of Light for about an hour just thrashing through how things might go down. I told him that Muzzy had told me to ask for £10,000 per week, so he used that as a starting point. He'd get me an appearance fee and win bonus, too. Cool.

Bob Murray, Sunderland's chairman at the time, was known as a tough negotiator. I went into the room initially, but there was a bit of a stalemate for a while. He didn't think I was worth what I was asking for, but Andrew was in my corner. 'Let's not talk about him like that while he's in the room – we'll take a break and sort it out afterwards.'

So my dad and I went outside while he took charge. Twenty minutes later, he came out.

'Well done, Matt – you've just signed for Sunderland.'

It was a great contract, and I was pleased that Leicester were getting good money for me. He'd got me £9,000 per week, rising by £1,000 each season for five years – so not far off what Muzzy had suggested going in for. There was a £100,000 signing-on fee on top of that, £2,500 for every appearance, a £4,500 win bonus, and if I started well,

£50,000 for an England cap. They didn't need to worry about that one in the end, though, nor the £25,000 I'd have earned if Sunderland had qualified for Europe.

'Now, if you and your dad could leave the room again please, I've got to sort out my fee.'

He'd been my agent for less than 24 hours, and I hadn't signed with him because I wanted to see how it went. If things stuck to plan – and that went for my career as a whole – I'd be with him for years to come. But shortly afterwards, he came out of the room and offered us both a celebratory meal on him. It didn't take too long to work out why.

'Andrew – you know how we talked about trust? I'd like to know what you got.'

And that's how to make £150,000 for less than a day's work. I couldn't believe it.

'I told you I'm good at what I do,' he said. 'But if what Ade's told me about you is true – and from the stuff I've seen so far, I believe it is – then I think Sunderland will be a stepping stone for you. You could be gone after a season for even bigger things, all being well.'

But I rang him the next day. Something just felt off to me.

'I know I'm only a kid, but that £150,000 isn't sitting right with me. My dad has been my agent up to this point, and my mum has always supported me since I was a kid. They've got absolutely nothing in this. I think giving half of that to them would be fair.'

I thought it was a reasonable deal. He'd been my agent for less than a day – it was easy money for him. And if he believed in me like he said he did, then I could earn him a lot more than that down the line.

'Give me an hour.'

And then the phone went dead. Later, he called me back and accepted it. What I didn't realise at the time was that the tax on that entire £150,000 from that fee had been written off in my name. At the end of my contract, I got a bill from the Inland Revenue for 40% of it – a cool £60,000.

The next day, I went back to Leicester to gather my things. Macca the kitman was gutted. He handed me a black bag, and I remember players coming up to me while I was filling it, asking whether I'd got what I wanted. I said yes.

'You can't argue with it, Pipes – that's football. Go and rip it up in the Premiership.'

I'd just signed a brilliant contract. But it didn't feel that way.

CHAPTER 11

Beckham's at the window

ONCE I knew there was no future for me at Leicester City, I didn't dwell on it for any longer than I had to.

I was genuinely happy to sign for a brilliant club like Sunderland, it had just been difficult to accept at first. Leicester was my home, where all of my family and friends were, and its football club was the only one I'd ever known since I was a kid. I'd just built up some momentum, the crowd knew what I could do, and now I would be starting all over again on Wearside.

But without a doubt, as soon as I got up to the north-east, Leicester were in my rear-view mirror. There was no feeling sorry for myself – it was like a new chapter overnight. Now, my life was about Sunderland and trying to do my best for them. But I knew that I had to start quickly.

My medical was basically a blood test to make sure I didn't have HIV or AIDs – I didn't have any scans. Twenty minutes was all it took. I remember saying to them, 'Is that it?' The doctor was just moving my knee a little bit, but there was nothing strenuous going on – it was so far removed from what a medical would be nowadays. He told me not to worry about some of my knee injury history at Leicester; that they had just been little tears, and that now I'd grown up with stronger muscles they probably wouldn't happen anymore. If only he had known.

As part of the deal, Sunderland put me up in the Marriott Hotel for three months, which gave me time to find a house. Stephen Wright had signed from Liverpool a few days earlier, so he was in there too. He knocked on my door and welcomed me straight away, and we were mates from the first minute. But Sunderland were desperate for a striker that summer, having finished 17th the previous season and scored only 29 goals all year. I know Peter Reid tried hard to get a rising Ajax striker called Zlatan Ibrahimovic before I came in, but for some reason he decided to stick it out for another year and sign for Juventus the following summer instead. Look at what he could have won.

Instead, Tore Andre Flo and Marcus Stewart joined nine days after I arrived. Flo's arrival in particular was massive for me. The £3.5m they'd paid Leicester made me Sunderland's biggest summer signing up to that point, meaning there was a lot of pressure on my shoulders. So when they brought Flo in for £6.75m, I was relieved. I didn't have to think about my own price tag. Generally, I always used to like letting everyone think I was on less money than I actually was. I knew other footballers who were the complete opposite, but I would always rather people thought, 'Jesus, he's only on three grand a week? So-and-so's on ten, and Pipes is playing better than him.'

I arrived into a dressing room of stars I'd been watching on *Match of the Day* for years: Kevin Phillips, Niall Quinn, Jason McAteer, Phil Babb, Claudio Reyna, Thomas Sorensen. They were big names. My first training session was on the Stadium of Light pitch, and I remember thinking that they'd all be looking at me to see what I could do. It's natural – that's just what happens when a new signing walks through the door. What's he like? What's he good at? Is he shit? Can he help us? They needed goals.

But it went well. I was confident, getting crosses in, shooting – it felt great. You could see the nods of approval, that they were accepting of who they'd paid a few million quid for. In the end, the likes of Quinn and McAteer were brilliant with me; Flo, too, who ended up struggling for goals and sadly had the crowd on his back early on.

Sunderland had drawn their opening game of the season 0-0 with Blackburn before I signed, but I couldn't wait for my debut against Everton a few days later – my first game at the Stadium of Light.

It came on 24 August 2002. I remember before the game, someone telling me that a 16-year-old might play against us

– and sure enough, he did. Wayne Rooney had just made his debut on the opening day of the season against Tottenham, and we both came on as substitutes with Everton 1-0 up. I thought to myself, 'Who is this young joker?' There he was, bouncing around on the sidelines, pure confidence. Not long after he came on, I tried to shoulder-barge him … and ended up in the advertising hoardings. I was four years older than him. Obviously we had no idea then that he would become such a superstar, but it was clear he had something about him. I couldn't do anything to affect that game, and we lost 1-0. Sadly, it would soon become the pattern of the season.

The biggest difference with Sunderland compared to Leicester was after matches had finished. We came out after that game, maybe an hour and a half after it had finished – shower, ice bath, rubdown, meet-and-greets with people you needed to see – and I swear there were still thousands of Sunderland fans waiting outside. At Leicester, you'd be lucky to get ten. They were calling your name, wanting autographs, and because I tried to be quite kind with my time, I'd be another hour doing all of that. Players wise up to it eventually as they get older, though – I've seen all the tricks. Sometimes, you ask the missus if you can hold your baby so you can get through without feeling so bad. I've even seen a video of Thomas Muller fobbing people off by pretending his passport was a phone.

The city itself was very different to what I was used to. You didn't see too many people of my ethnicity, but everyone was so friendly. They didn't even know who I was at first, but it didn't matter – it's just the way people deal with each other up there. You don't get that in too many other cities around the country.

I knew that Peter Reid was under a bit of pressure before I got to Sunderland, after the previous season's disappointments – a fan had even chucked a pint of beer in his face during a pre-season game. But like lots of other people, I looked at the players and thought there was absolutely nothing to worry about. It was also a massive squad with a lot of younger lads pushing through, so there was plenty of competition for places. When you go into a football club and immediately jump over young pros who are a bit older than you, there's often some bitterness. But thankfully, I never felt that at Sunderland. I'm not sure whether it was because of the price tag or what I did in the first few weeks of training, but it helped.

I was considered a first-team player, but because I was only 20, I ended up hanging around with the younger lads most of the time: the likes of Mark Rossiter, David Bellion (who later joined Manchester United), Tom Peeters, Michael Proctor, Kevin Kyle and George McCartney. There was a lot of good talent trying to push into that first team.

I started the third game of the season against Leeds at Elland Road – *them again* – but we won 1-0, with McAteer scoring just after half-time. I remember having to work particularly hard in that game, as we didn't have the ball much and Leeds were dominating … but three points were three points. Next up were Manchester United at home.

For the first three months at Sunderland, my girlfriend and I – she had moved up with me from Leicester – lived in Durham's Marriott Hotel, which is spread across a river with a glass walkway stretching over the water. The evening before a game, I used to like going for a walk around the town to clear my head and stretch my legs – so we did just that before United came to the Stadium of Light. I'd forgotten my phone before we left, though, so went back and left my girlfriend with a cigarette sitting on some steps, looking out across the river to the other side of the hotel. When I walked back, I could see she was completely and utterly transfixed by something on the other side of the walkway. I leant under the glass and could see it plain as day: a bloke standing there at his window in his pants giving her a little wave. As I popped my head out, the curtains snapped shut.

'Who was that?!'

'David Beckham …'

He was the person she fancied most in the world – I'd even bought her a calendar of him the previous Christmas. The next day, we played United and drew 1-1, although when you look down the team sheet again, I'll never know how.

We were 1-0 down after seven minutes through Ryan Giggs's early goal, but Flo equalised to get us a 1-1 draw in the 70th minute. Phil Neville was playing at left-back for United, and I felt like I had him on toast. I've always admired him and thought he was a good player, but I think with my style of play running him down the line and how strong I felt at that time, he couldn't get near me. He got booked early in the second half after chopping me down, and after that I knew he wasn't going to come near me. I felt like I was flying – any of the early worries about Sunderland fans taking to me had gone away. Once you know people are aware of what you can do, it makes your life so much easier. If you struggle from the start and then have to convince them otherwise, it's so much more difficult.

The standout moment of that game, though, was the flare-up between McAteer and Roy Keane, fresh from the fallout of what had happened during the 2002 World Cup with Ireland and Mick McCarthy. They'd been going at each other all game until Keane finally got sent off, after McAteer had wound him up about the autobiography he'd just released. 'Put that in your book,' he had told him after one of their earlier clashes, waving an imaginary pen. You can still enjoy that one on YouTube now.

I got Sunderland's man-of-the-match award, and Beckham picked it up for United. At the bottom of the

Stadium of Light tunnel, there's a lift you go up in to the room where you accept the awards – so there we were, together inside it. My first thought: he smelled amazing. Then I wondered if he'd remember what had happened the night before after seeing me … but there was no indication that he had.

'Well played today mate,' he said. 'After you.'

So, I walked out of the lift, and the room was absolutely rammed – everyone from the corporate section was in there. It was one of my first games for Sunderland, so it was all pretty overwhelming – everyone standing there cheering … until you realise it's not for you at all, but Beckham who's just strolled in behind. It was like waving to someone who clearly hasn't got eyes on you. There's no way to style that out. So I went up, accepted my award and enjoyed the moment anyway.

My other Beckham story comes a little later in life, but I'll tell it now. It made Mick McCarthy livid.

'Who the fuck is in that car there? Fucking outrageous.'

It was safe to say the gaffer didn't take a shine to my new motor. And honestly, I couldn't blame him either. There was a car dealer from Sunderland who used to come and watch our games – you couldn't forget him: he had a hook for a hand – and who also used to do a lot with Manchester United's team. At the time, Beckham was in Spain playing for Real Madrid. One day, this dealer came to a game while I was injured and asked me if I was in the market for a new motor.

'I've got Beckham's,' he said.

Obviously, that piqued my interest straight away. It was a Yukon Denali – this massive SUV, with blacked-out windows and spinning alloys. It was also bulletproof, with Beckham-branded initials stitched in gold on the inside. It was absolutely ridiculous. And I paid £50,000 for it.

I probably drove it no more than ten times because I was so embarrassed. You imagine rocking up at some traffic lights in Sunderland, with your wheels still spinning. That car just sat on my driveway for two weeks while I went out and bought a Mini instead. The final straw came courtesy of Thierry Henry, and a Renault Clio advert he did around that time. In it, he pulls up alongside an Ali-G lookalike in Las Vegas, driving a Yukon Denali with spinning wheels. He looks down, frowns, then laughs as if to say: *you absolute gimp*. I sold it the next day to someone for £50,000, on the proviso that I could prove in the logbook it had belonged to Becks. Thank God I could.

You had to have thick skin to survive at Sunderland sometimes – if you weren't having a good time, the fans would let you know about it. But I didn't actually mind that, because they were just honest with you. They wouldn't batter you for no reason, but if you were having a shocker, then they'd tell you about it. After that United draw, things went downhill very quickly.

We got fucking hammered at Middlesbrough in our next game, and I was booked within four minutes. Massimo

Maccarone knocked it by me and I wasn't having it, so I just took him out by volleying him across his legs. It was shocking, really – so cynical. He got his own back by putting Boro two up before half-time, and they won 3-0 in the end. In hindsight, I knew we'd be in for a struggle from that game onwards.

Another 3-0 defeat – to Fulham at home – came next, which couldn't have been any worse preparation for the big one against Newcastle at St James' Park. Reid had called me into his office the day before the game and explained that he was going to start me. 'But I want you to get your mind right tonight,' he said. 'You'll have never, ever played in a game like this in your life.'

'Don't worry gaffer, I've played Leicester–Derby,' I said.

After laughing in my face, he quickly moved on and explained why I'd be important the next day: that Sunderland would probably have to play a lot on the counter-attack, because Newcastle would have most of the ball. This was a really good Bobby Robson side that went on to finish third that year: Alan Shearer, Craig Bellamy, Gary Speed, Kieron Dyer, Nobby Solano – some big players.

'Don't worry gaffer, I'll be alright.'

Even when you drive to the training ground on the morning of that game, you're greeted by Sunderland fans with scarves and flags waving you on everywhere you go. There's a proper buzz, and it doesn't stop until you leave the city – fans are on the edge of the road virtually all of the way. The gaffer was right when he said I'd never experienced anything like it before.

St James' Park is one of those grounds where the bus drives under one of the stands to get into it. I was told that for most games they keep supporters back about 25 yards when the away team players get off – but it wasn't like that this time. Newcastle fans were right next to the bus, which was getting rocked from the start; singing their songs trying to intimidate us. As we got off the bus, there was only the width of a police horse separating us from them. You're Sunderland – they hate you. Then I got off with my little wash bag.

'Oi, Piper!'

I looked up between two horses, just as a Newcastle fan was brewing up a gob of spit to launch in my direction. And his aim was good – it flew through the air and landed just above my eyebrow. I lost it and tried to get at him, but the players and staff behind were just shoving me through to get inside. When we got in there, the gaffer sat everyone down.

'I told you what it was going to be like, fellas – this lot hate us. We're going to come here and do a job on them.'

It was a great speech which I can't do justice to here, but it got everyone up for it. I was still fuming, warming up absolutely livid, and the atmosphere even then was hot. St James' looks like it goes into the clouds it's so big, and almost everyone in there is getting on at you. The dressing room was quite small as I remember it, and you could hear the supporters upstairs stamping their feet when they knew you were down there.

Boom. Boom. Boom.

The game started, and in the worst way possible – Bellamy had them 1-0 up after 83 seconds, and we were up against it from the start. I got the ball a few times and stretched my legs past Speed, winning a corner. I remember the roar of the Sunderland fans when that happened; they went absolutely nuts. Sadly, they didn't have too much to shout about after that – it was 2-0 before half-time when Shearer rifled in a free kick.

It almost got even worse after an hour. Bellamy got the ball and came at me in the box, so I leant on him – I knew how quick he was. As he went down, the whole stadium erupted. I heard Mike Riley's whistle go and didn't even look at him – he'd given the penalty. We were already two down, and it was about to get worse, so in my anger I smashed the ball into the crowd and then went to argue with him.

'It's a free kick for a dive,' said Riley.

Oh. Even more fury from the Newcastle fans. Still: it finished 2-0.

Post-match, we got off that pitch as quickly as possible and into the changing room, where everyone was gutted. We got a knock at the door, and first-team coach Adrian Heath told me that I was wanted. I'd still got my shirt on, so walked over to the door to be greeted by two policemen. This day *could* get worse.

'Listen, there are no charges being pressed, but when you fired that ball into the crowd after the penalty incident, you knocked a 63-year-old woman out.'

Fucking. Hell.

Thankfully she was fine, just a bit concussed, but had spent the second half in hospital getting looked at. They wanted to know if there was anything that I, a Sunderland player, could do for her, a very angry Newcastle fan. So I took my shirt off, signed it 'To the lady I hit in the crowd – huge apologies, Matt Piper' and gave it to them. Half of me thought it was a nice gesture; the other half knew she'd probably throw it straight in the bin. But she didn't: the next week, it came back to me at the training ground with a 'return to sender' label. Fair enough.

After beating Aston Villa in our next game, we went to Highbury. I started on the bench because I had a niggle, but got half an hour at the end. I had massively looked up to Thierry Henry when I was coming through – I loved how he pulled left to pick up possession and make things happen from there. It's probably not so much fun when you're on the same side of the pitch trying to stop it, but that was my job – we had so little of the ball that I was coming back a lot to help out. All I could remember thinking was: *please, bro – don't burn me down the line*. I didn't want to get embarrassed. On that night, he feinted to do it a few times but then stopped and played it inside instead – probably because he just didn't need to, what with Arsenal being

3-0 up at half-time and basically taking the piss from there. Henry was ridiculous that season – 20 assists while also going for the Golden Boot with Ruud van Nistelrooy, eventually finishing only a goal behind him.

It didn't stop me trying it on with Ashley Cole at the other end, though. I got the ball two or three times in an attacking position and put the ball through his legs once, but he still managed to recover possession and then take it upfield as I tried to go around him. The attack broke down, and as he was jogging back he asked me, 'Bruv, did you just try to nutmeg me? Don't be silly.' I only played against him a few times – he's a year older than me – but he was one of the toughest players to get past without a doubt. Everything I tried with other full-backs just didn't work with him – he'd take the ball off you straight away. I know Cristiano Ronaldo also struggled against him during his days at Manchester United, so it wasn't too devastating.

Nine games into the season, we'd lost five and won only two. It meant that after seven years in charge at Sunderland, the gaffer had managed his last game for them. Reid got sacked in the international break that followed, while I was on duty with England's Under-21s for the very first time.

I was absolutely gutted … and things were about to get very uncomfortable indeed.

CHAPTER 12

Howard's way

I GOT into four squads for England's Under-21s – and never got an official cap. My first call-up came for a game against Yugoslavia in Bolton, and I dug out the team sheet for it the other day: it turns out that Nemanja Vidic and Milan Jovanovic (who later signed for Liverpool) were both involved on the other side.

But I couldn't get a look-in: David Prutton was the starting right-midfielder then, ahead of Shaun Wright-Phillips, Jermaine Pennant and me. I was very much fourth choice of that group. I was a bit pissed off, because I wanted to play for my country – that's what you dream of, ultimately – and would have been buzzing with 10 minutes off the bench.

David Platt knew Prutton, though, because they'd worked together at Forest. I'm not saying he wasn't a good player, but when you look at the three behind him, I can't believe he was making that starting XI every time. If I'm not getting in ahead of Wright-Phillips and Pennant, that's fair enough; I thought I was good enough to give them a push, but it felt from the start like I was almost a token pick – I'd gone to Sunderland for decent money, and they just acted on that to make up the numbers.

I don't think Platt really took any notice of me whatsoever, to be honest. I wasn't in his plans to start, so he didn't really make too much effort to get to know me. He had a brilliant squad, though – the midfield he picked for those Slovakia and Macedonia games had Michael Carrick, Jermaine Jenas and Joe Cole in it, while I'd been a sub against Yugoslavia with Peter Crouch, Joleon Lescott, Shola Ameobi and Matt Etherington. I didn't even make the bench for either of those other matches.

I heard about Peter Reid's sacking from one of the lads and I was gutted – he was the man who'd brought me to Sunderland, had been starting me regularly and liked what I was doing. Before our first win of the season against Aston Villa, he'd called me into his office for a little pep talk.

'Pipes – me signing you, and your performances so far, are what's keeping me in a job at the moment. Keep it up.'

Obviously it wasn't true at all and he'd only said it to boost me up, but it was short, sharp and brilliant management which made me feel 10 feet tall. So it was gutting to hear he'd gone – and it was just about to get so much worse. Three days later, Sunderland hired Howard Wilkinson as his replacement.

I was still with England Under-21s and was having a chat with Titus Bramble in one of the social areas when the news broke, and he slapped his forehead in horror.

'We've had him here with England before – you've had an absolute beast here. He's a fucking c***.'

But the nightmare was only just beginning. Not long after that, Les Reed, one of Platt's assistant coaches, came up to me.

'What do you think of your new gaffer, then?'

I puffed out my cheeks. 'I'm a bit gutted, Les – I loved Reidy, and someone has told me that Howard Wilkinson is a right c***.'

'Oh, really? No, don't worry – he'll be alright.'

I tried to keep an open mind about him while I trained through the rest of that under-21 camp, but didn't really know too much about Wilkinson. I knew he'd won the title with Leeds in 1991/92, that he used to be some sort of teacher back in the day, and that his nickname was 'Sergeant Wilko' – so I'd assumed he'd be a bit authoritarian. Apart from what Titus had told me, though, that was it.

When I headed back to Sunderland and prepared to meet the bloke I'd heard such a glowing report about, I tried to start in a friendly manner.

'How are you, gaffer?'

'Don't "How are you gaffer?" me. Get in my office.'

And that was my introduction to Howard Wilkinson. Welcome to the club.

'So I'm a c***, am I? I've known Les Reed for years, and he's told me what you said. I want to know who said it.'

'I can't remember, gaffer – someone just dropped it in conversation.'

'Look at you – you've gone away with England and put weight on. I know that under-21 lot and what they're like. You've not played and you have eaten four meals a day. If you want to get in my team, you'll have to lose some.'

I looked down, baffled – I was skin and bones. But he was hammering me. *What a start*. Despite all of that, though, he started me in his first game against West Ham – the perfect chance to prove the guy wrong and show him what I could do.

True to that season, though, we were 1-0 down at half-time: Trevor Sinclair had scored a brilliant goal, after a ridiculous 50-yard pass from Paolo Di Canio. As we got into the dressing room at half-time, Wilkinson walked in, slowly hung up his coat like he was trying to seduce somebody, and then told everybody to be quiet.

'You know whose fault that goal was?'

I was looking around the room thinking, 'Who's going to get a kicking for this? Micky Gray? Out of position, maybe. Could Thomas Sorensen have done better with it? It'd be harsh.'

'Fucking you,' he said, pointing at me. Di Canio had stepped off me to receive the ball for a throw-in, but there was no way I could have done anything to prevent what he did next – trust me, I've watched it back again just to check.

'No, I'm not having a laugh. Get closer to him. Stop him.'

'He's hit it over the oth…'

'Shut up – it's your fault. You know when I come in and say that to you? That means it's your fault.'

He was standing over me with his leg up on the bench, talking down and leaning on his knee. The next couple of minutes were dedicated to a speech hammering me a bit more, justifying his concerns about what I had allegedly done on England Under-21 duty and me trying to defend myself.

'You're not fit enough, I've already told you that. Might as well get in the shower – you're off.'

I was sitting there, wondering why all of the experienced pros sharing the dressing room with me hadn't said anything in my defence. None of them said anything, though, and that's when I first started thinking about football differently. There were some good lads in there, but football is for yourself to a large extent. If you're trying to get in with the new gaffer, you're not putting yourself in the firing line. But I didn't think it was fair.

My card was marked from the start, but I was only reporting back what someone else had told me. For an intelligent man, I always found that strange. Maybe it was because I never told him who'd said it.

Sadly, that West Ham game also turned out to be Niall Quinn's last for Sunderland – he'd been really struggling with a back problem, and decided to call it a day in November. He was a big miss for us – not only on the pitch but just for his overall presence in the squad.

Wilkinson didn't even put me in the squad for our next game against Bolton, then gave me 10 minutes off the bench in a 1-1 draw at Charlton. I was gutted not to start at Arsenal again in the third round of the League Cup – but as it turned out, that was probably for the best. Sunderland went in 2-0 down at half-time. Wilkinson's team talk was actually quite uplifting by his standards. He didn't batter anyone, and instead just acknowledged what a good team they were and explained how he wanted everyone to fight in the second half. And we did. He brought me on to have a go – beat players and get balls into the box – and it felt like the pressure was off. I was up against Kolo Toure, in his first full season at Arsenal, and did really well against him. We got back in the game and killed the crowd at Highbury: Kevin Kyle, only a couple of months older than me, scored our first not long after half-time and then Marcus Stewart equalised with 20 minutes to go. Two minutes later, we'd turned it around completely when I got down the wing and crossed for Marcus to head home. It was my best game under Wilkinson without a doubt – and I only played a half.

Positives like that, though, were few and far between. We hardly ran in training – it felt like we were barely doing anything. It was tedious. A lot of free-kick practice, a lot of corners – but not enough fitness work. We must have been so out of shape it was a joke – from what I can remember, there was just no high-intensity training at all. Instead, it was 'This is how we're going to set up here' – telling players which positions they should be moving into, and a lot about non-playing shape. Ask any player what they hate the most about preparations for a game and they'll say that. They don't mind doing it for an hour because they know it's important, but then at least finish with some proper football. Yet there he was, trying to tell me I'd got fat being away with the under-21s. At least I was running around with them.

The first thing that Wilkinson did was bring in an external company for some team-building exercises. We'd do trust falls with our team-mates, other exercises where you'd have to build the tallest tower from A4 paper, then one more where we'd all sit down in the dressing room with a bit of paper each. Everyone had to put their name at the top of it, and then you'd pass it round so that every player could write something positive about you on it. I remember getting mine back and reading things like 'quick', 'good team player' – then others that were completely useless like 'scored the last goal at Filbert Street'. The lads walked away from that wondering how it might help them score a

Premiership goal. I'm genuinely all for good team-building exercises, but they need to be done regularly for any effect – these just felt like desperate, one-off measures. You can't do a couple of trust falls and then expect to beat Fulham on a Saturday. I was only a kid at that time, but even then I knew it wasn't having the right effect.

But the best was yet to come. One day, Wilkinson cancelled training.

'We're not going out there today – we're going to sit in here and watch a documentary. I'm not going to tell you what it is, but *understand*: it's the team working together that will get us out of this predicament.'

So he wheeled this television into the dressing room, then hit play. David Attenborough's soothing voice filled the room, and he was talking about geese. We learned how they fly in formation and how when the leader gets tired, another takes over – that's how they can go so far for so long. I learned a lot about geese in that hour.

It didn't help us win any football matches, though. You can't just do that kind of stuff here and there, then expect the results to flow afterwards – it's got to be constant, and built into the ethos of what you're trying to achieve.

That Christmas, the gaffer said we were allowed to have a party, but it had to be a private thing because we were doing so badly – approaching mid-December, we'd won only three of 17 games and were only kept off the bottom of the table by West Ham. If we'd been caught out getting steaming, it would have been a nightmare from both the press and fans. So we went to this place called Bistro Romano in Cleadon. They knew all the players there on a first-name basis – it was a bit of a hotspot for taking out your wife or girlfriend. They said they'd close the restaurant for the night so we could take it over for the party.

We used to have this guy called Michael Price who travelled around with the team – he'd often be there standing in the background, and I didn't know who he was. Michael Gray explained that he was the man who looked after us on a night out – he'd been Arthur Scargill's No.1 bodyguard during his battling years against Margaret Thatcher. Pricey used to fight all over the world for money as some sort of bare-knuckle champion – he was absolutely massive, 6ft 5in of solid granite; the sort of bloke who wouldn't shake your hand but crush it.

I'd had a few beers that night and went over to say hello.

'Good to see you, son – not spoken to you before,' he said.

I asked him about Scargill and the bare-knuckle fighting which earned him his money. And then I did something really stupid.

'Michael, I'm not just saying this because I've had a beer – I think I could take you.'

'You cheeky fucker …'

And then he just switched. He grabbed me around the back of my neck, dragged me towards the door and out of the restaurant. My feet were basically off the ground at this point, and he chucked me out into the car park.

'Come on, then.'

'Mate! Michael! Pricey! I was joking!'

And then he grinned.

'Don't ever say that to me again, you little bastard – come here.' Then he got me in a headlock, rubbing my hair. I had an idea for him.

'I thought you were going to batter me. Why don't you go in and tell everyone that you filled me in out here in the car park?'

So he did. I stood outside peering through a little crack in the shutters, watching Pricey shadow swing and tell them what he'd done to me. I was waiting for everyone to rush outside to see what kind of state I was in, but what did they do instead? They pissed themselves. No one came outside. 'We knew he wouldn't have done you, Pipes,' they said. I wasn't so sure.

A battering from Pricey might have been better than what came next, though – the start of my injury woes that ended up plaguing me for three straight years at Sunderland. At first, though, it wasn't even my knackered knees: in November 2002, I needed a hernia repair which was only supposed to keep me out for a few weeks. I was pencilled in to return at Anfield and be in Wilkinson's team the following month, but slipped in my kitchen and set myself back months. Sunderland won 2-1 in the end, though, with Michael Proctor coming off the bench to get the winner 10 minutes from time. There was just one problem: that was the team's last league win of the season. It was the middle of December.

The atmosphere felt drab and gloomy. At Leicester, things hadn't been like that when we'd gone down – we were getting hammered every week but the lads were still in good spirits. For a while, there was a certain confidence that we could turn things around because we had good players. We had them at Sunderland too, but it just felt different – especially when Wilkinson came in.

I think the club saw very quickly that they'd made a big mistake. Nobody knows whether or not Reid would have got us out of it, but things wouldn't have been anywhere near as bad. The fans could feel it. No one stopped trying, it was all just … desperate. It stemmed from the manager with the one-off things he was trying, and then it transmitted to the team. Sunderland lost 15 straight matches to end that season, but I knew it was going to be all uphill after Middlesbrough in the fifth game. I didn't think we'd go down necessarily, but when Wilkinson arrived, that just confirmed it for me.

I know he said after his departure that Sunderland lacked leaders in their team, but I just don't think that was true. You look around that squad: Gray was captain, and there were plenty of other strong personalities in there: Sorensen, Babb, McAteer, Reyna. From what I remember, you got told if you weren't doing something right. McAteer was a big presence who I really liked, although the lads used to call him Trigger (after the *Only Fools and Horses* character) with good reason. The Pizza Hut story is legendary now – a group of us were there and he got asked if he'd like his pizza cut into four or eight slices. He said four, because 'I'd never be able to eat eight.'

Perhaps we did lack a bit of presence elsewhere, but I'll always look back at that time and question the manager. Football moves on – it's why for me, Sir Alex Ferguson is the greatest boss of all time. He rebuilt several teams and won over a number of years, even as the rivals around him increased in numbers and improved. Your new type of bosses – Jurgen Klopp, Pep Guardiola – have taken things to a different level with their philosophies, but you have to adapt again and again if you want to stay at the highest level. Wilkinson won the title with Leeds in a certain way – pre-backpass rule, for starters – and thought that could work again over 10 years later.

It didn't help that people weren't keen on his No.2 either, in Steve Cotterill. He'd resigned as Stoke boss to take the job, perhaps with the intention of doing what Micky Adams had at Leicester by stepping up when the time was right. But unlike Micky, he didn't have the kind of personality that players respected: he was smarmy, cocky and arrogant for the most part. Everybody knows that a good No.2 will strike a balance between being your mate and acting as a reliable go-between with the manager, but I didn't trust him one bit. If you said something to him, you could never be sure how he'd relay it upwards – and good assistants will always find a way of doing that.

Eventually, I did return to play some part in the rest of the season – but as ever, it didn't last. I got 20 minutes off the bench in my first game back at Tottenham, where we were already well on our way to a 4-1 defeat. The match before that had summed up that season neatly: Sunderland losing 3-1 at home to Charlton, with all three of the visitors' strikes coming via own goals in the first half. Poor Proctor got two of them.

In our next game, I came on at half-time ... but was praying I wouldn't have to. Sunderland had already been battered 3-0 by Middlesbrough earlier in the season, and were 2-0 down at half-time in the return game. Everything around the team was fury – fans had been ripping up their season tickets and throwing them on to the pitch in the first half. It was the most toxic home atmosphere I'd ever seen, and all I was thinking was, *do not put me on*. But he did, and we lost 3-0. I tried to ignore the dire situation by grafting, but the game was already done and they were smashing us to bits.

Our game against Fulham would be my last of the season before injury struck once again. Wilkinson and Cotterill had actually said they were impressed with what I'd done in difficult circumstances against Boro, and were going to start me. It was a difficult game for me on a personal level, though: the fans at Craven Cottage are right on top of you, and every time I got the ball, one bloke in the crowd was absolutely slaughtering me. When he saw that his insults weren't affecting me, though, they started turning into racial slurs. After the third or fourth time he'd had a pop in that way, I turned around and asked who kept doing it. As I peered in at the crowd, I could see so many black faces in there – it was horrific. 'How can nobody be telling this guy about his behaviour?' I asked no one in particular. But he just kept on doing it. We lost 1-0.

Thankfully, though, I'd played well. 'That,' said Wilkinson, 'is what I want to see more of if you want to play in my first team.'

It was the nicest thing he ever said to me.

Unfortunately for him, he wouldn't get the chance to dish out any more compliments – that Fulham defeat was the final straw for Sunderland's board, who sacked him and Cotterill at the half-time break of a reserve game they were both at. By 1 March 2003, the team were seven points adrift at the bottom with nine games remaining.

We found out the next day because Wilkinson had called a full staff meeting at the new training ground – it felt like everyone was there, including the reserves and young pros. He must have asked the chairman if he could tell everybody himself.

When Wilkinson arrived, he did the same as in that first West Ham game: walked in quietly, then slowly took off his coat, letting everyone wait for him. Cotterill was in the background with his head down; nobody could see his eyes. I vividly remember thinking how weird it all was – but for some reason, I still didn't think he'd been sacked. But then he spoke.

'Today is a very sad day for all of us: for me, for Steve …'

He was pausing a lot – you couldn't knock his ability to build the tension.

'I've been sacked as manager of the football club.'

I think everybody was a bit taken aback, and I wasn't even pretending – inside, I was having an absolute party. Apparently, though, I wasn't the happiest man in the room.

Tom 'Pepper' Peeters, a central midfielder who'd signed for Sunderland from Mechelen in 2000, stood up.

'YES! Get in there!'

He was still clapping when he sat back down, grinning like he'd just heard the best news of his life. I was leaning forward trying not to laugh, not quite believing that someone had the balls to do that in front of all those people.

'That's unprofessional – sit down,' Phil Babb barked at him. 'Shut up.'

But he just carried on whooping and clapping.

'No, no! It's brilliant news. Come on!'

I've spoken to Tom about it since – I was quite close to him at Sunderland, and he was treated like shit there in fairness. Wilkinson's approach was to make him train with the kids every day, and by that point he was a proper,

24-year-old pro. It can happen to footballers. Babb was the only one who spoke up at the time, but I know a few of the lads afterwards thought what Tom did was out of order. I liked those balls, though, and I could understand how he felt, having been cooped up for so long.

I think Cotterill had expected to get the top job at some point, but he was snivelling away behind Wilkinson in the background, probably wondering why he'd given up his job at Stoke to be a No.2 with us.

I'm sure Howard was a different man when he won the title with Leeds, but he came across to me as a bit of a dinosaur who didn't move with the times at Sunderland. He blanked those who weren't in his matchday squad, and if you were on the fringes, you might even just be training with the kids. He didn't want you anywhere nearby, and it didn't make for good morale. I don't think anyone ever thought he was a good fit at Sunderland – even him, by the end. He admitted afterwards that it had been a mistake to take the job. The only player I ever heard say anything nice about him was Babb, which surprised me given his experience. I used to hear that from him and think, 'How can you genuinely believe that he's a good gaffer?' I just couldn't see it, but it's each to their own.

Sunderland were sinking without a trace and on their way to plumbing new depths in the Premiership, but at least brighter times were ahead for them. If only I could have said the same about my own future.

CHAPTER 13

A hopeless cause

SUNDERLAND WERE well on their way to becoming the worst Premiership side of all time. I remember that being on the lads' minds, which can't have helped – ultimately, it's not the greatest thing to have on your CV.

I didn't think another team would be worse than that, but as I write this now, Sunderland's 2002/03 total has been lowered four times. The next side to break our record, three seasons later, was … er, Sunderland. But God bless Derby for their 11 points of 2007/08. Now I really don't think that will ever be beaten.

To be honest, I wasn't overly concerned about going down – it had been a horrible slog after another poor year the previous campaign. Mainly, though, I remember thinking straight away that the new boss Mick McCarthy was going to be a great manager for us. We were going down, but I backed him to take us straight back up. I was still only 21 by this point, but he was going to be my tenth manager in the space of three years – it was crazy.

He actually said to me in a steam room early on, 'I know about you Pipes, and when we get you back fit, we're going to have a good player on our hands in the First Division.'

He just wanted me to get myself right and not rush back, said some really nice stuff about what a threat I could be in the second tier, and that I'd be playing every week for him. He was the polar opposite to Wilkinson; with Big Mick, you were desperate to get back and play in his team.

He never beat around the bush with you, either. You didn't always know where you stood with Wilkinson, but McCarthy would always just tell it to you straight – and boost you if you needed it. He'd say things like, 'You didn't have a great game today, but worked hard after only just coming back from injury – well done for the effort.' You'd take the stick, no problems.

Unfortunately, though, there was no such thing as a new manager bounce for Sunderland when the gaffer took charge. He lost his first nine games to end the season, and we scored in only two of them. Despite the desperate need for more goals in 2002/03, the team had scored even fewer than the previous season – just 21 – on their way to collecting 19 points. It was bad.

I couldn't play in any of those matches, though. My hernia was giving me grief after that small run of comeback matches under Wilkinson, and despite returning to training before the end of the campaign, I had to have another operation – what's called an inguinal ligament release, which gives you more range. The first surgeon had repaired my hernia too tightly, so it was always pulling and causing me pain. The second doc opened it up again, took out the stitches and then put a gauze over the top of it.

My rehab was complete just before the summer began, but that hernia had kept me out for 23 games in my debut season. It was frustrating, but not soul-crushing – there was no reason to think that I wouldn't be back fit in the First Division. On the whole, I'd been pleased with my performances, and I think that was reflected by what other people were saying at the time. I used to be the sort of player who'd buy all of the newspapers to see what they were saying about me, although it would have been a nightmare if social media had been around – you read some of the abuse that players get now and it's horrific.

There were rumours that Leicester wanted to buy me back that summer for £1m; Micky Adams even came out in the press to say that the club wanted me back. They had just been promoted back to the top flight after a season in the second tier, and this time it was Sunderland who were having money problems – they were £30m in debt. I honestly had no idea about those rumours at the time, but I was genuinely happy at Sunderland by then. Clearly, they didn't want me to go anywhere because nothing happened – I think the gaffer really liked me.

Not that it stopped me from getting fined by him every now and again. Our goalkeeper Thomas Myhre used to have these small 'snus' pouches which were traditional in Scandinavia – they had nicotine in them, and you'd consume them by putting them between your gum and upper lip.

He asked me if I wanted to try one once, saying it would just relax me before training, so I said yes before I even knew what it was.

'What do you do with it?' I asked him.

One of the other Scandi lads said they were also good to put under your foreskin after sex, which obviously baffled me ... but just in the mouth would do for now.

'Better to use it before training,' he told me. 'It'll chill you out and make you play better.'

I took it just before I went to the toilet, reading the paper for 15 minutes before I went out to train. Everything was great, snus between my gums ... until I heard a knock at the door.

'PIPES!'

It was the gaffer. I sorted myself out quickly, went outside and asked him if I was late for training.

'Late for training? It finished 20 minutes ago.'

This snus bag had wiped me out for three hours. I told him what had happened, with the worst pins and needles in my legs that I'd ever had, but he wasn't exactly sympathetic: there went a chunk of my wages.

Thankfully, though, my inguinal release had genuinely made all the difference for my fitness – as soon as the surgeon had done it, I thought, 'Jesus, this feels good.' I did a week's training before everyone went off for their holidays and was basically fit to go. But even a relaxed break wasn't safe in the life of Matt Piper.

I went away to Portugal, but then started getting a pain in my testicle. I left it for a few days, but then woke up one morning and my scrotum looked like a grapefruit. I rang Sunderland's physio to tell him what had happened, and he told me to ring the surgeon. Immediately.

'Can you get a flight back today?'

So I did. Because of the plane pressure, I was in agony. When I got there, even he was shocked – imagine hearing, 'Jesus! You poor man' from a surgeon who's seen everything. It was badly infected. I'll spare you the details of what happened next, but let's just say the needle was so terrifying it looked like something you'd find in a fancy-dress shop. Just before the operation, though, I'd spotted a metal ruler on the side.

'You'd better not be measuring anything when I'm going in,' I told him, jokingly.

He laughed – but the truth wasn't far off. When blokes are getting operated on around their nether regions, they can often get 'excited' and make things more difficult for surgeons. That ruler is genuinely used to slap the misbehaving subject back to where it should be …

I flew back to Portugal, and within a week my poor ball sack was back to normal with the help of some good old seawater. *Surely* now, I was ready for a crack at helping Sunderland get back up to the Premiership.

The club had made plenty of changes over the summer in a bid to reduce the wage bill. Kevin Phillips, Tore Andre Flo, Gavin McCann, Jody Craddock, Thomas Sorensen, Bernt Haas, Claudio Reyna and Kevin Kilbane had all left for decent money; David Bellion, Jurgen Macho, Lilian Laslandes and Emerson Thome were all gone on free transfers; Stefan Schwarz had retired; even Micky Gray had gone out on loan to Celtic. It was a proper clear-out: in their places, only Gary Breen, Jeff Whitley and (later) Tommy Smith came in on free transfers.

After a niggle which kept me out for the 2003/04 opener at Nottingham Forest, my first game of the season came against my old club Mansfield in the League Cup – and I genuinely played brilliantly. I knew the kid who was marking me because he'd been in the youth team when I was there on loan. He was a good player, but a bit slow, so I just went at him all game. It felt good to be back, and we won 2-1 – Kevin Kyle scored an own goal for them to equalise in the 89th minute, then went up the other end to make amends and get the winner himself in injury time.

I started the next game, a grim 1-0 defeat to Millwall at the Stadium of Light which meant we'd lost our first two First Division games of the season, but then we won

2-0 at Preston to end that horrible run of 17 straight league defeats. We *really* needed it, as well: another loss would have matched Darwen's record of 18 in the 1898/99 season. I spoke to the gaffer about this recently and he told me it was his most memorable game in charge of Sunderland for that reason. I hit the post just after Sean Thornton had put us ahead, but we were two up at half-time through Marcus Stewart. Five minutes after the break, I was forced off with a niggle. I didn't know it at the time, but that knock would spark a chain reaction of events which sadly came to define the rest of my career at the club.

My knee had given me a bit of grief at Deepdale, but it was nothing too bad – the kind of problem that took a couple of weeks to get back from. So, on 10 September, I played in a reserve game against Blackburn to get a bit of fitness back, coming on at half-time after starting on the bench.

Jay McEveley was a strong, aggressive left-back who was only an 18-year-old kid trying to make an impression at his club back then. Maybe he was a bit over-eager to do well and show what he was capable of – but his actions more or less finished my season. I was doing well against him after coming on, and in a moment had beaten him for pace to put in a cross. I remember looking up at it, waiting for the ball to be headed … then *bang*. That shows you how late it was – I had time to watch the flight of the cross before he absolutely smashed me. My knee just locked at an angle and the physio realised straight away that my ligaments were damaged – it was a partial ACL tear.

I had surgery in October with a guy called Steve Bollen, who I'll always remember for his pair of Porsche 911 Carreras with 'ACL' and 'PCL' number plates. Rehab is pretty demoralising in that situation, but I always took it seriously with the physios: I'd come in early every day to get myself right, doing whatever they asked of me in the gym or pool. But the knee wasn't getting better – instead, it was just swelling up. I went to see Bollen again, who suggested upping the intensity of my programme. For a while, that was absolutely fine – I was doing things at half pace, then three-quarters, with no problems. I'd even started doing some ball work – the absolute indicator to show you're almost back – but then I blocked a shot in a 2-vs-2 session two days after Christmas and my knee immediately felt unstable. It swelled up again. Two days after that, I was back with Bollen having another round of surgery. I've still got his letter from just before the second op.

'Matt is still having problems, but then he has had lots of operations on his knee, a partial meniscectomy and now a partial lateral meniscectomy,' it read. 'The difficulty is knowing where to go from here.'

At 22 years old, I was already being treated as a lost cause.

It was around this time that we started to form a bit of an injury club. I got close to another young lad, Mark

Rossiter, who was a couple of years younger than me and had a tumour in his knee. It was so bad that he'd had to get a bone graft from his hip to reconstruct his knee, when he was only 19. So like me, he was out for a massive amount of time.

Mark had made his debut in that Highbury cup win against Arsenal under Wilkinson, and done really well. I'm sure that without those injuries he'd have been a great player, but he ended up spending the rest of his career in Ireland. I liked Mark from the start, and remember him saying to me straight away, 'Us boys have got to stick together up here.'

I wasn't sure what he meant at first. 'Well, I'm Irish and you're black.' He told me about those old signs you'd find on some windows in England: 'no Irish, no blacks, no dogs'. Obviously, he was joking: Sunderland wasn't like that.

We both worked really hard to get back as quickly as possible, but that was Monday to Friday. Those of us who knew we wouldn't be getting anywhere near the team on a Saturday used to have a bit of a Friday Club, where we'd go out and drink hard; two young, injured lads drowning our sorrows. We'd go to Frankie and Benny's and get smashed – I'd look forward to those nights. I'm a bad watcher of football if it's my own team – you feel worse when you can't be out there. I'd go to games but only stay until half-time, thinking that the gaffer wouldn't miss me. It sounds awful now, like I didn't care, but I just used to hate sitting there watching and feeling sorry for myself. I didn't go out drinking afterwards or anything like that – I'd just go home.

Everyone within the club knew I was one of the hardest-working players there – in at 7am, swimming every morning – but I found it hard. 'You're the fittest injured player I've ever seen Pipes,' the gaffer once said to me. But he also used to say things like, 'Fuck me – if you were a horse, you'd have been shot by now.'

It's fair to say I'd got to know the club's non-playing staff pretty well by that point. It's also fair to say that you *had* to know some of them before interacting properly. In my first week at Sunderland, I'd walked into the old training ground and introduced myself to the masseur, Micky Holland. I was first in after training, so I asked him if it was OK to have a massage.

'Sorry, mate – you obviously don't know how the rules work around here. We do the white lads first, then if I've got any time at the end, I do the black lads. Ask Phil Babb: he knows.'

I didn't snap – I was a 20-year-old lad still wet behind the ears – but I asked him, 'Are you taking the piss?'

'Mate, that's how we do it here – it's always been the same.'

Right at that moment, I knew it wasn't the time to kick off; I didn't want people thinking in my first week that I was a mardy bastard who couldn't take a joke. But he wasn't laughing, and he was being deadly serious. I just noted

My brother Dan and I: revving up for a wild ride at Wicksteed Park.

Me, bottom-left: Totally Dedicated to being a ball boy at Filbert Street (apparently).

The freezing indoor sports hall at Belvoir Drive. I'm the one buzzing next to David Nish (back row, right). The great Nev Hamilton is in the background.

All grown up in the youth team alongside the likes of Jordan Stewart, Matt Heath and Jon Stevenson. Jon Rudkin (middle row, right) was our loyal coach.

Loving life on loan at Mansfield, 2001 – even with the world's most pointless cup.

I gave Marcel Desailly the runaround when Chelsea came to town in February 2002. This was one way to stop me that afternoon...

The official matchday programme from Leicester's final game at Filbert Street, signed by all of my City team-mates.

The Hunchback of Notre Dame would have made heading look more graceful than me – but at least he didn't score the last goal at Leicester's famous old home. (Leicester City FC)

Enjoying my first City goal with team-mates (from left) Alan Rogers, Jon Stevenson, Paul Dickov and Callum Davidson. (Leicester City FC)

… and then just plain milking it. (Leicester City FC)

Turning out for Leicester in our first game at the (then-named) Walkers Stadium. Little did I know it would be my last for the club.

In the Tyne-Wear derby for Sunderland – never a penalty, ref. Thankfully not pictured: me accidentally knocking out a pensioner which immediately followed this.

A rare high at Sunderland: coming on at half-time to help overturn a 2-0 deficit and beat Arsenal at Highbury in November 2002. That's a fresh-faced Kolo Toure with me.

it in my head: I had a five-year contract at Sunderland – eventually, this guy was going to need educating. So I took it and walked away, feeling gutted. I sat in the corner, thinking, 'I'm going to start telling him as early as tomorrow.'

As I was sitting there pondering how I was going to do it, the door burst open and all of the lads came through pissing themselves.

'Got him with the oldest banter in the book! I'm only joking, son – get on the couch.'

I knew that was the best time to start. So I said, 'Mick, listen: I can take banter – but not everyone is going to act like I did. Some people will kick off. If you did that to some of my mates in Leicester, your jaw would have been on the floor.'

Every now and again we'd talk about stuff, and slowly I thought that I was getting through to him. Then, in February 2004, we signed Darren Byfield from Rotherham. Micky collared me.

'I've spoken to all of the lads – we're going to get him today with that same gag.'

'What have I been saying for the last six months, Micky? I'm telling you now: he's not the kind of character who'll just take that. Don't do it.'

So what did he do? He tried it – with a predictable outcome. Byfield had a swing at him straight away, then Micky went back at him. Darren didn't spend long at the club – only until that summer – but the pair of them never spoke to each other again.

I swear Micky earned about the same as the players did during his time at Sunderland. Amazingly, he was a massive Newcastle fan with the club badge tattooed on his leg, and he had a contact who sorted him out with all kinds of gear. Everyone loved him: despite some of the medieval jokes he still rolled out, he was a funny character. He'd come in with fake Rolex watches, fake Louis Vuitton handbags, Prada coats, boots, shoes – anything you could think of. If there was any deal going down where you could make money, he had his finger in the pie. I spent a lot of time with him, because during a week where I was injured, I was getting two or three massages from Micky per day. I counted that he'd probably made about £3,000 from players flogging the new stuff he'd brought in. He was a brilliant salesman. Lads would take cash in all the time; even the gaffers would be getting stuff for their wives. Because, who'd ever think that footballers would be wearing fake gear? I used to have all sorts.

After three more months of rehab, swelling, irritation and aggravation on my latest injury trail, I was back in action by March 2004. Sunderland were deep into their promotion push. I got 11 minutes off the bench in a 2-0 win against West Ham, but in our next game against Stoke, the gaffer put me on 10 minutes into the second half – we were losing 1-0, against a side featuring Gerry Taggart and

Ade Akinbiyi from my old Leicester days. He'd told me at half-time to keep warm, and had a word with me before I went on.

'Pipes, this is a big game – go on and do something for me, because we need this.'

At the same time, he brought on Byfield. Quite quickly, I started picking the ball up and going on runs; 15 minutes later, I put in a cross which Darren converted to make it 1-1. The knee was still feeling stiff, but everything else felt great after almost six months out.

Around this time, I had said I wasn't going to cut my hair again until the end of the season, by which time Sunderland would hopefully be back in the Premiership. I basically had an afro by then. After that game, the headline on a local newspaper was 'Hair today, top flight tomorrow'. The gaffer was buzzing with me – his whole speech after the game was basically about me. 'That's why I need you back in this team – get yourself fit, because we want to be playing up there again next season.'

Like I said, McCarthy was always great for a boost when you needed it. He'd say things to his players like, 'Fucking hell lads, nobody's getting near Pipes today. He's got the radar on.' Going back to one of the first training sessions I had with him, I genuinely scored one of the best goals of my life. We were playing a shape game that turned into an 11-vs-11, and I liked it if I was in the shadow team – there was that added pressure to perform and impress. In that match, I won the ball deep at right-back and then took off. I always worked best on instinct in those situations, where you didn't plan too much in your head. So, I just kept taking people on … and on … and when the keeper came out, I just went around him and rolled the ball into an empty net. After training, the gaffer said to me, 'You're the most expensive player we've got left, on one of the highest wages, and you're on them for a reason. Get fit – you're my No.1 player.' It made me feel so confident after another depressing period out on the sidelines.

Life changed for me in a different way on 9 April 2004, when my first-born Brandan came along. With all three of my kids, I just burst into tears in those moments – it's something that just always happened to me.

Even though I was a young dad, I knew that I'd always wanted kids from as far back as I could remember. Before you become a dad, you're told that it's going to be hard – but fundamentally, you know that you're always going to do your best, to treat them right and love them no matter what. When it happens, though, it's a strange feeling: suddenly, you have a new child in the world who is more important than you. You feel that unconditional love straight away, that you'd do absolutely anything for them immediately. It's very powerful.

I remember taking Brandan to the Stadium of Light when he was only a few weeks old – the players had a box they could use when they weren't playing. I opened the glass door as a roar from the crowd went up – at Sunderland, it's massive – and saw this little baby tremble in my hands, then burst into tears. It was the first time I made that connection to my dad protecting me when I was growing up, because it was exactly how I felt at that moment.

Back on the pitch, the team was doing well in the latter months of the season when I was back fit again, so the gaffer was mainly using me off the bench. Sunderland had also made the FA Cup semi-finals, where we'd be playing Millwall at Old Trafford – easily the biggest game of my career to date.

I remember my old man getting up to his old tricks. He approached Martin Tyler before the match and told him, 'My lad's playing today – he's been out for ages, so make sure you big him up please.' Tyler mentioned meeting my dad on his commentary later that afternoon, and how much it had made him smile. Shameless.

Pre-match, the gaffer played extended highlights from the 1973 FA Cup Final, when Sunderland had beaten Leeds for the club's last major honour – Jimmy Montgomery pulling off his unbelievable double save that was possibly even better than Gordon Banks's against Brazil. 'We want to be the next Sunderland team to win the FA Cup,' McCarthy said. I remember the huge effect it had on the lads, and how it put everyone in a great frame of mind.

So obviously, we lost 1-0. Tim Cahill scored the only goal in the first half and stood out for them that day – not just for that, but an overall dominant performance. It wasn't long afterwards that he got his move to Everton. I didn't come on for long – only 13 minutes – but the gaffer was going all out by that point. I didn't feel nervous, because I didn't think I had much to lose – we were already 1-0 down, so I could just come on and try to move the ball a bit. There was one moment where I saw the stars. I'd played a one-two with someone, about 30 yards out, then thought I'd chip one to the back post. But the defenders dropped deep, so I pushed it one more and then thought 'fuck it'. Sadly, I didn't catch it right. I was going for the far post with my laces, but scuffed it to the near post and the keeper, Andy Marshall, had to readjust. It looked like it was going in … but he managed to just about clip it around a post. I was gutted – that's the kind of thing which earns you hero status at a club. The Sunderland fans were absolutely unbelievable all day – the noise behind the goal that we were attacking in the second half blew you away. It was massively disappointing not to give them an FA Cup Final.

Around this time, we flew back to Newcastle Airport after a league defeat, and the gaffer wasn't in the best of moods. As we were walking through the terminal, a group of Newcastle fans started dishing out some dog's abuse at him.

'Oi, Mick! Fuck off out of our airport.'

He smirked it off at first, but they kept coming after him as a group. It felt like things could turn a bit nasty as more lads came, and one of them shouted, 'Stadium of Light? More like the fucking Stadium of Shite.'

The gaffer lost it. He threw his bags down and stood there with his fists up, while their main guy ran at him. People got between them before anything serious could kick off, but the group of blokes carried on following us and were growing in numbers. The players couldn't get in their cars quickly enough.

I was one of the last to leave. As I was getting in my car, I saw this giant geezer who'd been desperate to fight the gaffer, looking around the car park trying to find people. I turned my key in the ignition … and the battery was dead. I rang around trying to get people to come back, but none of them did. I could see the Newcastle fans searching cars, trying to find any obvious signs of Sunderland to give them an excuse to kick off and do some damage. So what did I do? I laid down and hid in the footwell so no one could see me, while ringing the AA to come and jump-start my car.

At least the blokes didn't spot me.

Thankfully, our FA Cup defeat to Millwall didn't immediately knock our automatic promotion hopes. I started the next game as we beat Wimbledon, then got rested for another win over Sheffield United. Sadly, a run of three straight defeats meant the play-offs would have to do – though I wouldn't be playing a part in them.

My last appearance of Sunderland's 2003/04 season came at Selhurst Park on 21 April. We were only 1-0 down against Crystal Palace when I came off after an hour, despite our goalkeeper Mart Poom having been sent off after 20 minutes, but we went on to lose 3-0. I was still trying to get back to full match fitness by this point, so played for our reserves against Everton six days later.

And then I waved goodbye to another nine months of my career.

CHAPTER 14

Over … and over

I TRIED to play on, but it wasn't happening. My left knee was in bits again after a tackle from Everton youngster James Potter. After hobbling around for 10 minutes, I came off the pitch knowing that I'd be gone again for months. If Sunderland did get promoted back to the top flight, I wouldn't be playing a role in it.

After the game, it was diagnosed as yet another partial ACL tear – one more to add to a pile increasing at a desperate rate. Sunderland didn't know what to do with me this time, so called it in straight to the top; in May 2004, they got in touch with Dr Richard Steadman, the legendary knee surgeon who had previously worked wonders for the likes of Ronaldo, Ruud van Nistelrooy, Alan Shearer, Lothar Matthaus and Michael Owen.

'In short, we have major concerns about his ability to play football at this level,' wrote our head of sports medicine,

Pete Friar. 'Matt appears to be at the watershed of his career and I hope something can be done which allows him to play a game at which he is very talented.'

It was a last roll of the dice. So, later that month, I flew to Colorado and went under Steadman's knife – sadly, not for the last time. There, he told me about my condition called lax ligaments which meant I never really stood a chance in football. When you stop at high speed to turn in a different direction, your ligaments are supposed to fire up and keep the knee joint in place. But because mine were lax, it meant that the joints slid around – especially as a winger, doing stuff at high speeds. Whereas other people's knee capsules might move half an inch and then click back into place, mine were all over the show. When you've also got a torn cartilage, there's hardly any blood flow to your knee, so you need an operation. You're out for months, back again, then exactly the same things happen. Steadman told me there was no operation that could sort my problem – you can't tighten ligaments. You can only work on your muscles to help do the ligaments' job for them.

At that point, I had no idea how long I was going to be out for. I went to Sunderland's home play-off game against Crystal Palace in May, where the lads went out on penalties and missed out on the Millennium Stadium once again. Everyone was wounded afterwards. I watched on as the gaffer did a rousing speech after that match, though, talking about going for it big time next season. He'd parked his emotions from the disappointment of getting dumped out in the semi-finals, and was focusing on next season straight away.

'We're not messing about with the play-offs next time, lads,' he said. 'We're going to win it and we are setting our stall out right now.'

But that summer wasn't much fun for me. I went to the Lilleshall Clinic for a week in June as part of my rehab, then had to continue working with our physio during the summer while everyone else was back for pre-season training. Steadman was sending through exercises and advice from Colorado, but coming back from injury is slow progress – it was three months before I was back doing anything like proper exercise. Every day, I'd go through the same tedious regime to nudge myself back towards training – and for what? It had happened so many times already that everyone knew a repeat was inevitable down the line. You start to wonder what your purpose is; what you can actually offer anyone as a professional footballer anymore.

Sunderland were desperate to avoid a setback, so inched me back towards action. I was in light training by late September, then in with the reserves by October. So far, so good – even if I wasn't allowed to train for more than three days at a time for a few weeks. By mid-November I was playing for the reserves again – and that's how it stayed until January. On New Year's Day, 2005, I finally pulled on a Sunderland shirt once more, starting again at Deepdale against Preston.

And I was absolutely shocking. The gaffer dragged me off at half-time when we were 3-0 down to a Richard Cresswell hat-trick, and butchered me in his fury. But Gary Breen stood up for me. I always had a lot of time for him – he was a great lad. You'd have never known it from looking at him, but he'd grown up on the streets of Camden and was a tough bastard.

'Fuck me, Pipes – you've been out for ages, you're a top player,' McCarthy started on me. 'I give you an opportunity … and then you turn in a performance like this.'

Breeny called him out, defending the time I'd been out injured and wondering why he wasn't having a pop at anyone else on the team. In the moment, I thought back to that West Ham game when Wilkinson had dug me out in front of everyone and no one had said a word. I always respected Gary for doing that.

Still, Mick might have had a point: in the second half, Sunderland scored twice and the final score was a more respectable 3-2 defeat. From then, they only lost two more games across the whole season and absolutely smashed it to win the title.

But my season was over as quickly as it had begun. I made three appearances across eight days in January 2005 – all short ones off the bench – and that was that. Nothing was amiss after we'd beaten Palace in the FA Cup; I played

90 minutes for the reserves and went about business like normal.

Then, suddenly, the knee pain returned. I got my heels clipped in training, and the agony was back. I was a footballer who couldn't be tackled – already feeling completely useless, having just turned 23. It didn't matter how hard I worked in rehab, or how much I wanted it: I was gone. I look back through my injury records now and it just seems a blur. By that point, I think I was starting to wonder whether I even cared about playing anymore. Even if I *did* get fit again, did I want to be out there putting myself through it? You can see now how games become a chore: hating everything about the build-up to them, knowing you'll never ever build up a rhythm and any kind of confidence.

From January onwards, I was just an expensive pin cushion: injection after injection for months on end; exasperated letters of disappointment from experts unsure of what to try next. It was like trying to keep a broken egg together with sticky tape. To give you an idea, here are some excerpts from my injury files, January 2005 to that summer:

Jan 19: Returned to training.

Jan 28: Knee pain returned.

Jan 31: Improved, may be able to train.

Feb 5: Knee remains sore, some improvement but unable to train.

Feb 8: Injected with a sugar injection.

Feb 10: Knee OK, pain gone after injection.

Feb 12: Feels stronger.

Feb 14: Improved knee stability.

Feb 17: Sore medial ligament.

Feb 18: Medial ligament remains sore.

Feb 21: Ball work, weights.

Mar 1: MCL pain gone; Roger Oldham for injection in left knee.

Mar 5: Joined in training, non-contact.

Mar 14: Played 60 mins for reserves; blocked ball with right foot. Managed remaining 60 mins. Sore medially and laterally afterwards.

Mar 15: Blocked a ball, now has medial pain in right *ankle*.

Apr 15: Sore today, compression.

Apr 20: Not to play tonight in reserve game, still sore when striking ball.

Apr 25: Played full game for reserves.

Apr 27: Still sore, not playing Thursday.

Apr 30: Settling down nicely.

June 27: Returned from break, ankle still sore. Had sugar injection to right knee over break, to see Dr Oldham again this Friday.

June 29: Sent for MRI, slight thickening over ATFL in ankle.

July 1: Steroid injection.

July 9: Feels back to normal. Still having injections both knees. Oldham says to keep out for longer because of injury history.

July 10: Full training with reserves, no reaction.

Aug 28: Aching knees.

Sep 13: Mild discomfort.

Sep 15: Played full game but took heavy tackle, ankle sore after game.

Sep 16: Another injection.

It makes for depressing reading. Amid all of this, I also had a blazing row with the gaffer, which didn't help. I'd been out for ages, and the club had organised a behind-closed-doors match to help a few players get back to fitness. McCarthy asked me to play, but I told him that I couldn't.

The physio at Sunderland was unbelievable with me over those years, but because I'd been out for so long, he thought there was a bit of a mental block holding me back. He wasn't sure whether the pains that I was feeling were just in my head. The gaffer had been relayed that information, and was trying to force me into playing.

'Gaffer, I'm telling you now – I'm not.'

'Get your fucking boots on and get out there – you are playing. It's all in your head.'

I stood strong and we went back and forth for ages, but there was no way I was going out there – those pains were not in my head. He snapped, and so did I.

OUT OF THE DARKNESS

'Fuck this,' I shouted, then got in my car and drove home. I was clearly losing the argument with him, and didn't want to carry it on anymore. Halfway there I felt guilty and contemplated turning around, but thought I'd look like an idiot going back straight away. In the end, I just went in the next day and spoke to him. He was cool about it, but fined me. As it turned out, they did a scan that week and did find another problem after all.

Sunderland had done absolutely fine without me anyway. After their title win, the gaffer came to me and said, 'I'm going to give you a medal. You've not played enough games, but you've made a big contribution within the squad.' He must have just felt sorry for me – but it was the kind of guy he was.

That summer, I tried to do my own bit for the club. I still had two years left on my contract, but they were still struggling financially. I felt like a fraud earning money from them while I wasn't playing, so agreed to defer £100,000 of my salary and a £50,000 signing-on fee – extending my contract for one more year, but for no extra money. It took my weekly wage down to just under £8,500, which was still massive in the circumstances – and earned my agent another £10,000 for the privilege.

I went away with the squad on their pre-season tour of the USA and Canada that summer, covered in bubble-wrap once again. I couldn't play in the last two games because they were on artificial pitches and could have ruined any number of my body parts. It was a good trip, though, and I was able to show glimpses of my old self. McCarthy gave me the No.7 shirt again, and told me I'd be one of his starters. By then, it was a miracle he had any faith left in me.

But I knew things still weren't right. If it wasn't my knees, it was my ankle – the injury I'd picked up in April was still giving me grief by September, and I was still having regular injections just to get me through reserve games. It was relentless. And it was finally the end.

I made one appearance for the club in 2005/06 – my last ever game in professional football, on 20 September 2005. It came in the League Cup against fourth-tier Cheltenham at the Stadium of Light, and I remember it all clear as day.

I didn't feel like a footballer anymore. I was absolutely awful. Even people who I'd got close to and wanted me to do well knew it too, no matter how kind they were trying to be and acknowledging that I'd been out for ages. After the game, one of them came up to me and said, 'You didn't look right.'

It felt like things had changed. I knew I'd been out for a long time, but I told him he was right – it really didn't feel good. Everything felt too quick. That standard of player – no offence to Cheltenham – was taking the ball off me so easily, and I found it all a major struggle. I felt like I'd lost pace, lost some of my tricks, my quality on the ball – all of it just gone. I'd never felt like that on a football pitch before. I came off after an hour with one thought: *that's it*.

It wasn't quite over in a flash, though: what happened next was an utter piss-take. Two days after the game, I woke up with a huge nosebleed, and went to see our club doctor who couldn't stem it. They even ran tests on me because they thought something might be seriously wrong. The next day, the same thing, and the day after … until finally, they stopped. It was almost comical. My ankle was still a mess, but they didn't want to operate on me because of all the injections. By the end of October, they had no choice – it was back to Bollen for more surgery. Someone had to pay for those Porsches.

More rest. More rehab. More problems. A panic attack. The end.

The injuries were very real – it was one thing to another. I wasn't feigning any of them.

By the end, I'd learned how to be fine with accepting notes that simply said, 'Needs surgery'. As soon as I knew I'd be out for a certain number of months, I felt better; much better than when I was coming back and waiting for the next thing to go wrong. I had become a professional injured person, and was more comfortable with that.

But I'd got tired of having to wonder what came next. I could have sat on my contract and kept picking up my wages for two and a half more years, setting myself up for a comfortable retirement. Technically, I was still owed over £1.1m in wages alone by Sunderland – but I didn't deserve it. I didn't care. When the chance to get out for good came along, I grabbed it as quickly as I could.

At the start of January 2006, I'd even spent two weeks at Coventry – then being managed by Micky Adams – with a view to them taking me on loan. But I just didn't want it. I didn't want to be a footballer.

And so, weeks later, my life as a pro was over by the age of 24. I was so desperate not to be that guy anymore that I settled for a quarter of what I could have got. My agent was telling me to just stay put, because the club would keep upping their offer to get rid of me. Sunderland had seen how desperate I was to finish, though, so originally offered me £200,000 and my playing registration (meaning I could sign for someone else as part of the settlement). For a while, they played hardball – and even tried some reverse psychology, telling me to just stay for more rehab. But I'd already started getting excited about what could be next – like a lot of footballers, I hadn't really thought about what was coming on the other side, but had been thinking about starting businesses.

I didn't fancy a major fight with Sunderland – they were struggling and weren't going to come up with much more. In the end, we settled on £300,000: £100,000 up front, and the rest to be paid in £10,000 instalments for 20 months. I knew that I was shocking with money – if they'd given me everything in a lump sum, it wouldn't have been good for me at all. It was still less than half of what I could have got, but I wanted out. They accepted it, but wanted to hold my registration. My agent said no, and after a bit of back and forth, they gave up. By then, me going in any way at all was a good deal for them.

The gaffer had been great about it with me all along, although my cynical side knew it would have been a relief to get shot of me. I know he was being genuine when he wished me good luck. On my last day, I said goodbye to him and the kitman, John Cooke, who played for Sunderland back in the '70s and '80s and had joined the staff in 1994. A proper legend. Kitmen are usually the people players get closest to. They know all the little secrets of the dressing room, and they're good at keeping them. The ones who can't don't last long, because players will get them out quickly. It's why Macca is still at Leicester, too – he's respected. They come to you on your last day with a big black bin liner full of shirts, shorts and boots. It's like the last day of school.

I remember walking around Sunderland's training ground pretending to be gutted because my football career was over, but inside I was excited about what might come next. There's a part of you that's numb, don't get me wrong, but looking back now I think that's just the ego – you finish, and you're not a footballer anymore. You don't walk into a room and it's, 'There's that Sunderland player.' When you're done, you're done.

I've got to admit, I felt that. I think it's another area that footballers don't really talk about much: losing that feeling of walking into a supermarket and noticing people whispering around you. There are levels to how much that affects people. Tony Cottee, for example, is one of the nicest, most humble blokes I've ever met in football, but I bet even within him there's a part of him which misses that part of the game.

But I wanted my freedom more. It's going to sound ridiculous, but I also wanted to call it a day there and then so I could go on a snowboarding holiday with my brother and some mates in Chamonix. They used to go every year, and I was always gutted that I never could. It was more or less the first thing I did when I finished.

I'd never been skiing before – every footballer's contract bans them from almost every other activity – so I hired an instructor for the day. I'll never forget his name, because he was such an arsehole: Philippe. Because of how I was as a footballer, it was so frustrating not being able to get it straight away. All of my mates had gone up high into the mountains, while I was stuck at the bottom with this guy. I was going down the small slopes, falling arse over elbow and getting back up again. Then repeat.

'You know Matthew, some people just can't do this.'

'Are you having a laugh? I've paid for the whole day – I'm not giving up.'

'Yes, but you're not getting it. You can't do it.'

It reminded me of being a kid. You'd have to wait ages for the ski lift to come back down and take you up again, but I just kept grabbing the board and sprinting back every time. After about six hours, I finally went from top to bottom without falling. *Philippe, mate: I'm going up that mountain.*

'You're not ready. You're not ready ...'

I was ready. When I got up there and went for it, I was going full board – my knees were in pain, but the pure release of everything that had come before was more important. You go back up to the top to have some beers, then do it all over again. I really needed that.

So there I was, perched at the top of the Alps, squinting into the sunshine with no worries. There was another life out there to live. I had truly closed the door on football with one thought: *let's have it.*

And that's where my life went crazy.

CHAPTER 15

Lost in the world

IF ANYONE had tried to offer me advice about what to do next after retirement, I probably would have paid lip service to it. In one ear, out the other.

The PFA gets a bad rep from some ex-players, but I know how difficult it is for them. I didn't want any support at that time. Anyone who is forced to finish professional football early gets a pay-out of £25,000, so I tried to get that as soon as possible. You're supposed to receive the money to tide you over while you move into something else, but really I just wanted it as soon as possible so that I could make a clean break.

There are a lot of footballers who think that the PFA could do more – and I'm sure for some, they could – but it's difficult for them when they encounter attitudes like mine at that point.

I thought I had plenty of cash in the bank, that I was in a good place to make the next thing happen for myself, and that everything would be OK. At that point, there was no reason to think otherwise: I was 24 years old with the rest of my life to live.

The first thing I tried to do was sort through my finances – but in hindsight, I wasn't really equipped with the tools to do so at that age. I had five properties when I was a footballer, two of them in Sunderland, and put one of them up for sale straight away. My mum was living in the other one down the road from me for a while, having moved up there when she'd split up with my dad for good. I sold one more of my houses down in Leicester, took a lump sum out of my pension – which you could do early, as it was a footballers' one – then pooled all of my money together.

When I collected everything, I remember looking at my assets and thinking, 'Fucking hell, I've got £700,000 here. I'm fine.'

The thing was, though, that my bills were probably still £8,500 per month. And what did I do about them? Very little, to be honest. Because I didn't sever or manage my high-cost outgoings as soon as I'd finished playing, I was only seeing a fraction of my monthly £10,000 'earnings' from Sunderland. I didn't pay any of my main mortgage off in a lump sum.

I thought I was set for an insurance windfall, too. My agent had set me up with a policy for the length of my five-year contract at Sunderland, to give me a £1.8m pay-out if I had to finish within that time. But there's always small-print. When I filed for it, they cheerfully referred me to the section which made the whole thing void if I was finishing because of a body part that I'd already had three operations on. I tried to take it to a tribunal, but didn't get anywhere near – I barely had a leg to stand on.

But I thought that I was going to be alright: I could do *something* here. I had financial advisors, but stupidly, my money disappeared down to virtually nothing in less than three years. Advisors were putting my cash into things that were making *them* money. One of them, who looked after a lot of footballers, invested some of my money into all sorts of things, but he inputted the address for my paperwork wrongly, so I was getting some of the correspondence instead of him. I opened one of those letters once and saw that for one of the pots alone, he was making a lump sum of £17,000 for about 10 minutes' work. All he'd had to do was tell me that loads of people were doing it, and making good money off it. I never told him that I'd seen the letter, but I used to question him every time after that.

And thank God I did: one day, he came to me with another scheme that a lot of high-profile individuals were getting involved with – film partnerships. The idea is that you put your money towards a movie, which becomes a tax write-off as a creative cause. When the film comes out and starts making some money, you can earn four times back what you put in. Now, years later, everybody who got involved in that scheme is getting stung for tax they didn't pay in the first place – some for millions of pounds.

I can't remember any specific thinking along the lines of what I wanted to put my money into – and that was a huge part of the problem. I was going on a lot of holidays I probably shouldn't have taken and blowing silly cash down in London, where I'd think nothing of spending thousands on a table in a club.

I knew I had to do *something*, though – I just didn't know what.

So I tried all sorts of things. I started doing some work for Leicester City in the Community, going into schools and doing bits for them. At that point, though – completely unlike now – I didn't really enjoy it. One of my other mates who I used to play football with at Leicester had started a call centre business that was doing well, and suggested I become a salesman for him. So I tried it for a couple of weeks, shadowing him while he tried to sell phone lines into companies, but I knew it wasn't for me. Then I went to work with another mate who was a builder, doing a bit of labouring for him to help out. After that, I tried my hand at carpentry and tagged along with an electrician friend, but my feelings were the same. I was trying all of these different things, but didn't enjoy any of them.

I was quickly becoming a lost soul, as my life after football started to unravel. At that point, I felt like I'd lost my identity but was still trying to cling on to the lifestyle of a footballer. Mentally, it was conflicting.

I started to get this strange feeling that I'd never experienced before: one of unease and dread. It was like I didn't quite belong anywhere at that point, and with every thought I had, there was a level of darkness there. I went to see the doctor, who told me that I was suffering from depression.

My mum had grown up with it, so I already had some knowledge, but it's not always easy to identify within yourself when you've never experienced those feelings before. It felt like the world was closing in – I was getting apprehensive and nervous in situations that had never posed a problem to me before. The doctor put me on some tablets and said they would take some time to kick in.

I'd also go out at the weekend and drink, which made me feel better. The clouds lifted, and it didn't matter that I wasn't a footballer anymore. There were no dark thoughts, I was dancing … and happy. Ultimately, though, that's how drink tricks you when you're in a depressed state. You wake up the next day and feel even worse, so return to the thing that you believed was helping you in the first place. Every time I was a little bit tipsy, that easiness returned. But it's a vicious circle. You begin to drink every day, and then suddenly, that dependency takes a hold of you. You *need* alcohol to make it through.

I'd get to Monday and try to keep some sort of a routine, but really just be thinking, 'What am I going to do today?'

When you're struggling to find something you're good at or like, weekend drinking starts turning into Sunday drinking. Then Monday drinking. And that's how the snowball began. I was getting steaming multiple times per week. Everything was a release just to make me feel something good.

I also had the first fag of my life on a holiday in Marbella. My relationship had broken down by then, so I was single. I met a girl out there who asked me if I smoked – and to impress her, I said yes.

I coughed through the first one, but my addictive personality took control: an hour later, I'd done ten. I would get home from the buzz of those trips, and everything would just seem so depressing.

When I moved back to Leicester, my dad and brother were living in my old house. At that time, I had two properties on the estate I currently live on – one of them that I'd tried to make a bit of a footballers' crib, including a cinema room. I sold that one, though, so only had one decent-sized house left. I rang my old man and told him that I was coming back to live in it. But I should have known it wouldn't end up well.

Little things started getting on my nerves; he was treating me a bit like a kid again, changing the channel to things he wanted to watch when he got home from work or asking me to turn the music down.

'Dad, this is my house – I'm not 14 anymore.'

One day, I said that to him and he got angry. He'd grown up in a household where the child was expected to be obedient all the time, and he still wasn't at a point to let that control go.

We ended up having a massive barney about it. The argument carried on upstairs, and it got to the landing. My brother isn't a violent man at all, but he knew it was about to head that way. He tried to shout out for us to stop, but Dad was having none of it.

He ran at me, and I put him on his arse. He got back up furiously, spewing patois and calling me a *rasclart*, then went at me again. The same thing happened. It was the first time I'd ever done that, the first time I'd ever been the big man in the room when he was there. After that, he backed down. My brother was the mediator, and told us in no uncertain terms what he thought of us both.

For a few days afterwards, Dad was very apologetic – but I knew it wouldn't work with us all living there together. Something like that would have flared up again. But I loved him, and always will, so helped him out by paying for some of his rent towards an apartment of his own. Eventually, he moved into one of my other houses and stayed there for much longer.

My mum was always brilliant, but she loved me that much that she would say anything to make me happy around that time. I was spending money too freely, wanting to visit places flying first class. Everybody else thought it was a mistake, but she'd tell me to go for it and that I only lived once. But that's my mum – and I absolutely love her for it. It was only because she wanted me to be happy. I'm not sure tough love would have even worked: I became very good at telling those who tried that where to go. They weren't my mates, I thought. They didn't love me.

I'm not sure people know about this, but I even had a serious chance to go back into professional football at Leicester when Rob Kelly was manager. Because I didn't know what I wanted to do, and my knees were feeling alright – a bit stiff and sore, but nothing major – I rang the club physio Dave Rennie and asked him if he could check me out at Belvoir Drive. As he was looking at my knees and doing his tests, he told me, 'Mate, they're not that bad you know.' But he said that I was a stone overweight. And what Dave didn't know, because I hid it very well, was that I was smoking about 20 cigarettes per day. People like my dad were horrified – I had been such a clean-living player. Even when I turned up at Leicester I had a fag on, shovelling down mints and mouthwash to cover up the smell before going to see Dave.

Then he came to me with an idea: why didn't I come in for a bit? He'd train me for a while so I could shed some weight, and he wouldn't tell the manager – he'd just say I was trying to get a bit of help with some fitness. He was very close to Kelly, and said the manager would definitely have a look at me. So, Dave worked with me for about a month – my knees felt fine, I'd lost that weight, I was running OK … but I was still smoking. Otherwise, though, I was moving towards training with a Championship team – and it was going well. Dave was doing a bit of ball work with me, my touch was good, and I felt sharp.

'I think it's time to talk to the gaffer,' he said.

In my first proper training session, I was nervous. But I was a bit more a man of the world by then, and they weren't the stresses I'd remembered from before. It had just been a while, that was all. And then the first ball came in – someone whipped a really quick cross into the box, and I ran on to it with Patrick Kisnorbo marking me. It was behind me a bit, but I jumped in the air and backheeled the ball towards goal, off the post and in. It honestly felt like training stopped for a second; people were like, 'Shit, he's actually decent.' After training, Kisnorbo came up to me and said some really nice things to me, including: 'Bro, you can't retire from football.'

So I continued training for a while, and was loving it. I stopped smoking, started taking things seriously again, and was at Belvoir Drive for maybe a month, working every day. Kelly was making noises about making something happen behind the scenes, but tempering expectations by saying they'd only take me on a short-term rolling contract. If I got seriously injured again, the club would be gutted. I understood – I was fine with it. It got closer and closer, and Dave was telling me, 'The manager's going to offer you something – you're looking good.'

Around that time, in December 2006, I gave an interview to the *Leicester Mercury*'s Lee Marlow, which turned out to be a sign of things to come. People knew I'd been training with Leicester by then, but it was all pretty harmless – nothing more than getting a bit of fitness back. Some people really wanted me to make a comeback, but I'd paid for another operation with Steadman months earlier – £6,000 at my own expense – and he'd told me there was a definite possibility that I could spend my life in a wheelchair if I pushed things too far. Lee asked me what lay ahead.

'I don't know how you're going to write this one,' I told him. 'It's not straightforward. I wish it was. You keep asking me what I'm going to do – and the truth is, I just don't know. I wish I did.'

I can't remember what it was exactly – a stag do, I think – but there was something in the background at the time of this proposed return at Leicester where I thought, 'You know what? I want to do that instead.' But I knew I couldn't while I was playing football. The idea of being a footballer again just niggled away in the back of my mind. Suddenly, I started going in and complaining about my knee. Dave couldn't believe it. He was trying his best, reassuring me that it was only a niggle, but I couldn't give him what he wanted to hear.

'It's not going to work, Dave.'

And that was it.

I've got no regrets about most of my football career – not after what happened at Sunderland, because my injuries were genuine. But that one? It wasn't feigned, because my knees were sore, but that was my opportunity to carry on playing football – at Leicester, my hometown club. And I didn't take it. Loads of people were telling me not to go back. They thought I'd left on such a high by scoring the last goal at Filbert Street, and said I'd never beat that again. The injuries might strike. I might just be shit.

And it got to me. I didn't want it. Part of me just wanted to leave things how they were.

I definitely don't want people to think that I didn't re-sign for Leicester because I feigned injury. But, when it got closer, I just felt that pressure again – especially at my hometown club, where I'd done so well before. It wasn't worth risking all of that.

Around that time, Nigel Clough also rang me from Burton. They were only in the Conference, but he said to me, 'Matt, you don't even have to train. We just need someone with your profile to get the ball, run down the wing and cross it into the box. I know you can still do that – come to training.' But it came at a time when my drinking was taking over. My lifestyle had changed, and I didn't fancy that regimented routine of a player again, even at Conference level.

I trained at Mansfield for a while in the summer of 2007, but never had any intentions of signing for them. Part of me thought it might be great to go back again when I didn't have anything else going for me, but I'd only gone there as a favour to Billy Dearden, who'd returned as manager. I was pulling up to training with a fag on in my car – it was ridiculous. One of my biggest downfalls in life has been not being able to say no to people. I just didn't fancy it.

At that point, I didn't like anyone saying no to *me*, either. The lads I'd grown up with were all trying to keep me in check. 'We don't need to go out tonight – we can just go to the cinema or get some food.'

I was the one saying, 'Come on, that's boring – we're going out.'

I became very good at manipulating people to get drunk with me, just to serve the new habits – I knew that drinking was the only thing capable of lifting me out of my despair back then. When my proper mates didn't fancy indulging me, I'd just ring other people: the sort I knew, but wasn't necessarily friendly with. You could tell they were wondering why I was calling them.

My mates were being sensible, but I was pushing them away. I fell out with a lot of them over that time and it was all my own fault. I used to get the right arse with them – I'd say if they weren't coming out with me, then I'd just go on my own. The first few times you use that one as a manipulation trick, they relent. When it doesn't work the third, fourth or fifth times, you think: *fuck it, I'll go without you, then*. And I did – loads of times. I used to drink in the house first and then go out a little bit later when I was tipsy, often to a club called Basement – an after-hours place in Leicester that didn't close until about 6am. I'd turn up good to go.

But some of the things that started to happen after that got embarrassing.

This one time, a girl at the bar came up and started talking to me – it was just friendly chat, but you could tell these other lads nearby had tried it on with her earlier in the night first. They kept looking over until one of them came over and said to me, 'Come on – move over now. I was talking to her.'

'Mate, let the lady talk to whoever she wants to,' I said back to him.

So he offered me outside. By that point, I was annoyed and pissed – so I took him up on it. Because the club was underground, you needed to walk upstairs to get outside. The first pathetic argument was about who would go up them first, so you could see the other person. I grabbed the bloke and put him in front of me, following him up behind, thinking about how I'd try to swing at him first and get a good punch in. We didn't even make it to the top. Before that, he'd turned around and smacked me straight in the nose, sending me down the stairs bruised and battered. I was bleeding from a cut on my head and the poor girl at the bottom was telling me that I needed to go home. So what did I do? I went back inside, sat at the bar and got more steaming.

Sadly, it wasn't the last time that I ended up on the wrong side of someone's fists. After another night out, I was in a taxi on the way home, around 5am. I asked the driver to stop at a 24-hour petrol station so I could buy some more booze, and there were two scruffy-looking lads inside with white powder around their noses. Even in my state, I thought it was probably safe to assume that they hadn't been enjoying the free packets of sugar on offer. As I was waiting to pay, I picked up a coffee napkin and told one of the lads that he might want to wipe the cocaine off his nose – all very harmlessly.

'Cheers mate,' he said, then took it from me and did his deed. Out of nowhere, though, his other mate turned around and smashed me in the side of the head, sending me straight into a chocolate stand. The lad I'd given the napkin to then headbutted me in the face, shunting me back into a stash of crisps which spilled to the ground. They kept going at me; soft drinks and milk cartons flying everywhere. It was an absolute mockery in there.

I was swinging back trying to fight, getting nowhere, while the poor attendant was screaming for everyone to stop. The two lads legged it before the police came, but I stuck around – quickly sobering up – to watch the CCTV footage with them. We actually laughed about it as we watched, it was that ridiculous.

'What are you doing with yourself?' one of them asked me.

I told him I wasn't doing anything.

'Oh, you're unemployed.'

Well, I used to be a footballer ...

They're sitting there as strangers, giving me life advice. But it made no difference to the pattern of behaviour I'd got myself into. I didn't like what my world had become – the unfairness of it all, in my own mind. I couldn't find a job, my money was running out and I wasn't good at anything other than football. That was my identity, and it was gone.

This was when the clouds started gathering above me. I started to feel cloaked in failure and worthless as a human being.

Could it get much worse? Answer: yes. Yes, it could.

CHAPTER 16

Rolling in the gutter

WHEN THE clubs weren't open on a midweek night, I needed to find something else that might feed the habit.

That's when I started going to the casino regularly – more for the social and drinking side of things, rather than gambling, but still going on my own. I'd set my alarm for 1am, then drive into town.

I was terrible at betting. I used to play blackjack a lot, poker and roulette too, just getting steaming and burning my cash away. The amounts I lost weren't high-rolling levels – at the very worst, probably £2,500 in one night – but when you're doing it four or five nights per week, it turns into a very expensive hobby. Then you'd stumble outside into the light, drunk and dissatisfied – I never came out of that place sober.

These days, I go absolutely nuts if I hear about people drink-driving – but in those dark days, sometimes that fucking idiot was me after nights at the casino. Most nights I got a taxi home, but there were times when I didn't think it would affect me. I am far from proud of it – in fact, I look back on those decisions now with utter shame. In my current work for Leicester City in the Community, I visited a prison recently and got chatting to a lad who looked out of place in those surroundings. He'd gone out with workmates one night, driven home drunk, fallen asleep at the wheel and killed two students in a parked car. It changed his life forever.

But that's where my head was at by then – a dense fog that clouded my judgement and made me ignorant of consequences. One time, things went too far. There was this pub on a bend near to where I lived, with an eight-foot brick wall in front of it. It was raining at about 4am one morning when I came around the turn, skidded off the road and smashed into the wall. The car was a total write-off. I got out of it, ran home and got into bed. Just left it there. Steaming.

Later, I got a knock on my door – it was one of my neighbours. They'd come home from a night shift, seen the damage and heard the music still playing inside my car.

'You need to go and move it – I'll help you,' he said to me. 'Have you been drinking again?'

So we went and found it. The car had a flat tyre – the least of its concerns, frankly – but we began picking up all of the pieces from the road and throwing them into the boot. My neighbour took a sweeping brush to tidy up the mess, then drove my car back up to my house and parked it on the drive. He tried to give me the talk – it wasn't right what we'd done; I needed to get my life together; I couldn't keep going on like this. He'd have been well within his rights to have called the police right there and then.

I told him I would sort myself out. I went back inside to sleep.

Another time, I woke up on the floor of someone's house, half-naked, with absolutely no clue where I was. I remember coming around and looking at their pictures on the wall, recognising absolutely nobody in any of them. No one else was in the house. I looked out the window and saw my car parked outside, nudged into a skip with the back end dented in. *What the fuck.* I managed to find my clothes in various parts of the house, then just got in the car and went home.

In these worst times, I would get up at 11 each morning to watch the *Jeremy Kyle Show* – that was one of the things I had in my routine, along with the *Real Housewives of New York*. So I'd be there at home with the dog, getting smashed at my own pathetic house party with MTV Base. Every day, dancing around the living room with my poor boxer Kai, who didn't have a clue what was going on.

At that time, I had people checking up on me who knew that things were bad in my life, just popping round to see how I was doing. I'd be hiding drinks in cupboards, in the garage – anywhere to hide the evidence. They'd ask me if I wanted a cup of tea, but it was obvious they were looking for signs of booze.

I was on and off with my ex-partner during these troubled times, but each of my three boys were conceived in love when we were trying to give things another try. It might not have been destined to work as a relationship in the end, but out of it came the most important people in my life who make me so proud today.

Brandan was very young when I finished in the game, while my second son, Finlay, came along a few months after it was all over, in April 2006. When Kairo was born in March 2009, I was at a very low ebb and in no condition to look after a new-born baby. Luckily, though, his arrival was the point when I knew I had to get myself right.

Those boys were my light in dark days. I was still seeing them regularly with my mum during the hard times, but it was tough not being with them every day. I'm very open and honest with each of them now about my life back then, though, and they know what happened around my struggles after football. Thankfully, those experiences didn't shape me as a father or a person, and my kids know now that I'd be there for them in any situation, anywhere. They're the absolute world to me.

The truth is, I didn't really know myself back then. I got to 24 still desperately trying to work out which direction

I wanted to turn in next, but I had so little life experience in reality. The only thing I knew then was that I was a footballer. Before that? I was trying to be one. I didn't know myself without that identity. That's when routine falls away, discipline goes out the window, and I was all over the place.

You're waiting for something to drop into your lap – that's the problem. You sit there thinking, 'If this happens, I'll stop the drinking.' But that's a ridiculous thought process. You're in no position for something to just come along; you're not being positive, not being proactive and not working towards anything. What was going to come my way when I was sitting around the house, drinking myself into oblivion while watching Jeremy Kyle dress people down on TV? It could have been me on there.

One night amid the madness, my phone was dead because I hadn't charged it. People's calls were going nowhere. I'd gone out for an afternoon session in the casino on that occasion, stayed through the night, and nobody knew where I was. They were scared something bad might have happened to me.

At about 3am, I was playing poker and remember seeing my dad peering through the window – he'd been searching around for me, and my brother had suggested I might be there. He came in and just asked me, 'Are you alright?' Obviously, I told him I was fine. 'We've been trying to ring you all day.'

My old man didn't know how to deal with it. He was never shy of telling me what he thought when I was a kid, but with this, he didn't have any answers. There was no bollocking, no tough love. He just walked out in quiet disgust, because he didn't know what else to do.

'As long as you're alright,' he said. 'See you later.'

Towards the start of my spiral, I bullied Jon Stevenson into coming down to London with me. I give talks quite regularly now, including ones about mental health, and use this story to illustrate how badly out of hand my drinking got. I can look back at a certain period of my life and pinpoint where my behaviour became alcoholic.

My grandad, Uncle John, was ill and living alone at this point. I fancied seeing him and staying in London for a while, so I rang him to see if he would be up for letting us stay with him. I wanted a change of scenery, but also knew he'd appreciate a bit of extra help around the house.

I asked Stevo if he fancied joining me – he was also out of pro football and probably going through similar difficulties himself. Growing up together in Leicester's academy, it was clear that we had a relationship like brothers. He told me that he used to look up to me, but at this point, I was setting no good example for him. He was in between jobs but I told him not to worry, that I'd pay for everything. I just wanted someone to come with me.

My grandad had three bedrooms in his house, so we took one each. We probably ended up outstaying our welcome in the end, but I always tried to see Uncle John right and give him a few quid to enjoy himself at the bookies when he wanted it. He loved his gambling, but was the sort of bloke who could do his brains on £1.20 a day if he needed to – a few pence on a race here and there, to last the whole day.

We were going out every night throughout that period, and Uncle John would make us a fry-up every morning: West Indian style, with all sorts on there. With it – because he'd done it himself for years – he asked us if we fancied a little shot of whisky to ready us for the day. Before I knew it, doing that for six weeks, I became dependent on that shot to get me going. That's the point when things really started to go wrong. When I came back to Leicester, I was doing it every morning.

One night, we were out in London and neither of us really knew where we were: central, east, west … none of it really mattered. It was the early hours and we were starving, so went into a tiny Subway to get some food. It was packed with loads of people, but I started getting a bit lairy with the server who ran the restaurant. When we got to the till, he was being blunt with me – as anyone would have done when they had a clown in there acting up.

'You've been taking the piss – we don't want people like you in here,' he said.

Eventually, he refused to serve us. There was a huge bloke in there who looked like Anthony Joshua – he must have been 6ft 6in – and told me I was embarrassing myself.

He was right, but back then, people who told home truths like that were nothing more than nuisances. Stevo, all 5ft 8in of him, offered him out. The bloke behind the till screamed at us to get out, then called the police claiming that one of us had a knife.

We didn't, but he knew they'd come quickly if he said that. But there I was, smashed out of my face, trying to be the big man I thought I'd become … still demanding my food. The other lad had the good sense to scarper, leaving us to stick around until the coppers came.

'ON THE FLOOR – ARMED POLICE!'

They cuffed us, put us in the car and took us a few miles down the road before letting us out. We went home – the first sensible decision we'd made all day.

The next night, we were out again – to a totally different club, in a totally different part of London. Or so we thought. When we went to get food at the end of the night, we saw the bright lights of Subway once again … only to discover it was exactly the same one, with our irate friend going nuts at us to get out as soon as we'd walked through the door.

That time we did, but instead of getting food and calling it a night, we decided to try another club instead. At the place we'd chosen, you could only get in if you bought a table – and we didn't fancy queueing alongside the suited-up stockbrokers already there. I went up to the bouncer and asked him to let us in. We could go in the VIP area, he said, but it was £1,000 for a table. It was at this point he realised how drunk we were, as I stumbled around trying to move the barrier. As I lifted it up, I fell backwards and took 50 metres of rope with me into the gutter. People in the queue were pissing themselves, Stevo included. I was squirming around on the ground, trying to get up and failing miserably. The bouncer was vindicated.

'Look at you – there's no way you can come in here.'

But amazingly, we did – the girl next to him with a clipboard took our side, clearly desperate to take £1,000 from this pathetic human lying in a gutter. What we didn't realise until getting in there, though, was that they'd halved the size of this club with a black curtain so it looked busier – it was a midweek night, after all. And this is how bad we were: think Del Boy playing it cool in *Only Fools and Horses*. As we leant on what we thought was a wall – this black curtain – we both disappeared through it. A neat summary of those six weeks in our lives.

I didn't really recognise my alcoholism then – I thought I was just having a good time after my football career was over – but Uncle John's shot of whisky started giving me a little kick up the arse to start every day. I'd get a little buzz and want to keep it going. When 12 o'clock came around, I'd tell myself that I could have another one. Stevo and I had no plan of what we wanted to do in that period, living day to day.

I found that people almost went out of their way to help me at that point. They accommodated my behaviour, not because they were going to gain anything from it, but because they were afraid I'd push them away altogether and then they would have absolutely no control over what I was doing. Mum and Dad didn't really know how to handle it – how could they? – and neither did my younger brother, who had also always looked up to me when we were growing up.

One night, though, my brother decided he'd had enough. I remember this one like it was yesterday, because it's the most hurt I've ever been in my life. That feeling stays with you. By this point, Dan had met Laura, the woman who he'd later end up having my wonderful niece Luna with; they'd been together for almost a year and moved into one of my houses together. He had a full-time job.

I'd got home from the casino very late on a midweek night, bored and still drinking, so I rang him. If you get a call at 3.30am from someone you suspect of being an alcoholic, you immediately think of trouble.

'What's the matter? What's happened?' That's exactly how he answered the phone.

'Nothing, brother – just rang for a chat,' I said to him, giggling.

'It's 3.30 on a Thursday morning. I've got work in three hours. What are you doing?'

'Forget about that, mate. Let's have a chat.'

'You know what?' he said. 'Sort your life out. You're an embarrassment.'

I hammered him on the phone. In my woeful state, I couldn't believe he'd spoken to me like that. I was so close to him, and it felt like a dagger. So I told him I was going round there.

'Do what you want.'

The first time I ever got tough love, I lost my mind. I got in the car and drove round. He lives on a one-way street, which I went up the wrong way with my music blasting, got out and started shouting on this terraced street. When he didn't reply, I started banging on the door. *'Say it to my face ...'*

All I remember is the curtain from my brother's bedroom being pulled back, and Laura giving me a look of absolute disgust. She shook her head at me slowly, in a sad kind of way. Years later, she told me that my brother was petrified at that moment – me, head absolutely gone with nothing to lose, rapping on the door like I could come in at any moment. It destroyed him.

I'll never forgive myself for that, either. In Dan, I've got the greatest brother I could wish for – my absolute best mate, who is loyal, loving and humble. We grew up so close, and I treated him in a shocking way during those times. Thankfully, the kind of guy he is means our relationship became as strong as ever after I came out of rehab – he's a brilliant uncle to my kids, and an all-round amazing guy who I'm proud to call my family.

At this point, though, I was a lost cause. When you're in a situation like this, you blame everybody else for your own actions. When you're suffering from an addiction, nothing is ever your fault. *My younger brother talking to me like that, when I've just rung him for a chat? He must be mad – I don't care what time of night it is.* Blame isn't with you, so it doesn't affect you one bit. You're not thinking like a sane human being. It's only years later, when you're compos mentis and you realise: fucking hell, I can't believe I did that to my brother.

I was so wrapped up in my own misery that I don't even remember feeling embarrassed about what I was doing. It just got worse. I started experimenting with drugs throughout this time, smoking cannabis every day. It accelerated my downfall and destroyed my already-fragile mental state, without a doubt. It's not the same as getting drunk, because weed can make you such a paranoid person; it changes the chemical balance in your brain and you can become even more reclusive.

When you have no focus anymore, you start living in your own head. The idea of coming into contact with people became horrendous. Often, I just wouldn't go out of my house – not even to answer the door to the postman, who I was friendly with. I'd miss deliveries just because I didn't want to sign for them – anything to avoid showing myself to another person. If I did go out and come back while my neighbour was around, I'd return their greeting without even looking at them just so I could get back inside the house quickly.

Sometimes, I'd just pass out on the spot – it happened three times that I can remember. I was so conscious that some of the things I was saying to people might make them think I was a weirdo, analysing absolutely everything, that it could just become too much. It's even worse when you've got a personality like mine: if you add weed and drink to the mix, you can become so self-critical and paranoid. I'd be having conversations with people while feeling like a panic attack could come on at any point. Your heart starts beating faster, you begin to sweat, and that only makes it worse. *People are going to think I'm a fucking idiot. Why are they looking at me like that?*

Then … boom. Lights out.

One time, it happened at the gym. An older bloke started speaking to me in the steam room, while I still had the influence of weed in my body, so I began to worry that my responses to him were being construed badly. I could feel the attack coming on … then the next thing I knew, he was standing over me, gently slapping my face.

'Are you OK? We need to call a doctor.'

He went and fetched me a Lucozade to help raise my blood sugar.

Another time, I was at an Anthony Hamilton concert, dancing around a little bit drunk having also smoked some weed. I was with good friends who I felt comfortable with, but there were some people in front of us who it felt like, in my distorted mind, kept turning around and looking at me. Whether they were or not, they didn't really have much choice after I'd endured another one of these episodes and passed out on them. They were trying to push me off, not knowing I was out cold, but a security guard had spotted it. I got thrown out.

The last time I remember, I was at home on my own. I don't know what triggered it, but I just woke up face down on my floor nursing a giant bruise. The only previous time I'd suffered a similar incident was in that swimming pool at Sunderland – before my life had spun out of control.

As much as I tried to cover things up, the people closest to me knew I was in a terrible place. My mum would come in every day to check on me and just sit in my living room, crying. All I thought in those moments was, 'Please leave, so I can carry on drinking' – I was that lost. My old man mostly stayed away because he didn't know what to do or how to make things better.

I lost touch with most of the people I knew in football. When you jump forward a few years, thankfully I've reconnected with a lot of them, and they all say the same thing: they didn't ever know I had a problem. I didn't tell anyone because I didn't *want* to be in contact with them at that point – I had nothing good going on to talk about. There was only one time I really did feel embarrassed about my situation, and that was at Neville Hamilton's funeral. By that point I'd put a lot of weight on and stopped playing football, and knew I'd have to answer the same question:

'What are you up to now?' I must have looked like an absolute joke. His death really affected me.

I even managed to upset one of the few close mates from football that I had left. Brian Deane had always been a bit of a father figure to me, as I discussed earlier, but he rang up one day and gave me an absolute dressing down. A really good friend of his had approached me in a club one night, and I took a joke a bit too far with her. At the time I didn't think there was anything wrong with what I'd said, in my pissed state, but it upset her. Deano rang me the next day and told me straight up what he thought – another one of the few times I got some tough love. Obviously, I blamed it on the drink.

When you can't sleep at night because your thoughts are racing and you're paranoid about everything, you need a different kind of drug to counteract the cannabis and booze. Whether it was sleeping tablets or Valium, I wasn't fussy.

The first time I ever took Valium was before all of my problems started. I went to the doctor and told him that I hated flying – at that time, I was genuinely petrified of it.

'This will calm you down,' he told me – and he was absolutely right. It's a drug that takes the edge off fear. The first time I took Valium, I absolutely loved it. I thought, 'Wow, this is an amazing drug.' All of that anticipation, fear, those nerves … it just suppressed everything. It shuts your thought processes down and helps you sleep. So in my desperate times of need, I remembered the drug that had helped me out before.

I went back to the doctor and told him that I needed some more Valium for a long aeroplane journey; multiple flights, so I would need quite a lot. It fooled him. *No problem, here's a nice big prescription for you.* Every time I wanted some more, I'd just go back there and tell him a different story. He started to warn me that he'd need to stop giving it to me, but all that did was make me more manipulative. I told him that I could easily get it online; that if it wasn't the original stuff and made me ill, it was on him. He wasn't happy, but he signed off on one more lot anyway.

'Don't be trying those tactics again,' he told me.

I did. Every single time, I'd try to get him with a different story – sometimes I'd even cry in front of him, saying I'd probably kill myself if I didn't get what I needed. Inside my head was not a nice place to be at this point.

It's hard to say now exactly how much whisky I was resorting to each day back then, but it was probably around two litres. I was definitely seeing off more than one bottle each time, at a litre apiece, but there were containers with different amounts in all over the house. When you've got those alcoholic tendencies, you'll always want more. If I'd finished one by 11pm, I'd just go searching elsewhere to top me up. I knew the situation was bad when the bloke behind the petrol station counter grabbed the usual two bottles for me before I'd even gone inside the shop.

This was what my life had become. And when you're sinking without a trace, at some point you'll find the bottom.

CHAPTER 17

Knockin' on heaven's door

WAKING UP felt like nothing.

These days, I get out of bed with a purpose: not least for my three sons and step-daughter, and being a good husband to my wife. What makes me happy now is knowing that people can look at me and feel both trust and love. I do my 45 minutes of exercise as part of a routine, and then I'm into my day.

When you're in a bad place, the bottle becomes your routine. I feel sick talking about it now, but I was in such a mess that I couldn't see what I had in my life. From the position I'm in now, and the person I am today, I'd always point someone who was struggling in the direction of their family. Think about your kids; think about everyone.

But how I was back then, it felt like a whole lot of nothingness. You're sitting there drinking whisky at ten o'clock on a midweek morning, you've learned how to roll a spliff, your highlight of any day is trashy TV – and yet you are still intelligent enough to think: this is fucked. Why aren't you trying to get yourself together? Your brain is telling you that, yet you're doing the opposite.

I remember once sitting there, crying, telling myself: get yourself fit. You think that once you're there and you've stopped drinking, you can start to sort through your life and focus on the things that really matter. Then, you can get a job. I had all of these building blocks in my head. People might read this and think what a loser I was – but that was just the low point I'd reached. You feel disabled when you're lost to addiction.

It's very hard to explain to people who haven't been in that situation before, because on the surface it's quite simple: why don't you just go and get help? Some of it is being scared to ask. A lot of it is still believing, right up until the last moment, that you can turn things around yourself and not burden everybody else with your problems. All the while, though, you're trying to do the same things and expecting a different outcome – it makes no sense. Running was a building block towards moving out of that space, but at that time, I just didn't have the strength to carry it any further. That's why I think it's so important for people in that situation to seek help: it's not just talking things through and finding the root of your issues, you also get equipped with the tools to work out coping strategies. It's like building an armour around yourself. You understand more about what others are going through, and how you aren't alone. You're taught to be more proactive, rather than reactive, and that's very important.

Sharing with others is also huge. In rehab, they teach you that if you can share with a stranger, you are helping them too. Just listening to someone else is productive. I share a lot on social media now, which I do to help others – but I also do it to help myself, based on what I've learned.

I later discovered the thing that was messing me up most – more than the booze, more than the weed – was Valium. I was on 80mg a day when I eventually went into Sporting Chance – that's eight pills per day. The recommended daily limit is 2–10 mg, two to four times a day, but only on occasions you really need it. By that point, the doctor knew I was addicted and told me he couldn't prescribe any more. So I just started buying it from America in bulk, which is scary – people have died from doing that before, getting something that wasn't the legitimate product. And it was expensive, too: about £10 per tablet; 30 tablets for £300. Imagine how regularly I was buying that stuff, as another hidden cost of my addictions.

I'd spent my last £140,000 doing up the house. I had a huge tax bill when I retired, but there were other huge things I cleared off as well: a few credit cards with £20,000–£30,000 on them. It didn't take long for the money I'd earned from my non-playing contract at Sunderland to disappear with my monthly outgoings. I'd given a fair chunk of cash away to help family members out, even though they'd never asked me for any of it. I hadn't come from anything, so it didn't bother me going back to having nothing again. Money is good in a way that you can do what you want when you want, but it doesn't instantly make you happy.

My Valium habit built up over time, but I was probably taking those pills regularly for a year and a half. If I took 80mg of that stuff now, I'd be slurring all over the place – you just can't function properly.

I started doing some commentary for Radio Leicester at a fitting point in Leicester City's history. Like me, the team was sinking to new depths: in 2007/08, City were on their way to the third tier of English football for the first time ever, under Ian Holloway, and my performances behind the microphone were even worse. I was on the whisky, on my pills – and on course for disaster.

This neatly sums up why I didn't think I was an alcoholic at that time: if I knew I was on commentary that day, I'd stop drinking at 6am that day *to be professional*. Still hungover, still feeling shocking, still popping pills to counteract the nerves of going on live radio. My speech was slurred, my thought process was non-existent, and sometimes the commentator – now my good friend, Ian Stringer – would come to me at vital moments for my contributions and I'd look at him with fear and dread, making cutting gestures at my throat because there was nothing in my head. *Do not come to me.* Ian would just have to keep speaking and making things up, game after game.

I'd become a master liar. Ian would ask if I was OK, but I'd just tell him I'd been out the night before and had a few. He's an intelligent and assertive man, but I could fool anyone at that time. He'd had no idea that I was thinking about suicide and in utter despair. You would never be able to tell, because the sufferer becomes far too good at hiding their true self. Needless to say, I only lasted a few months – I was awful.

I was also doing some work for the PFA, where I'd go and commentate to a student who was in a studio somewhere, typing out what I'd said to track games on a live blog. I used to take my mate with me and sit in the press box at Leicester with a flask by my side. Everybody thought it had coffee in it, but it was just straight whisky. My mate couldn't believe it.

'Pipes, there's not even steam coming off it.'

I was oblivious at the time, commentating while smashed out of my box on booze and Valium; some poor kid on the other end of the line wondering what the fuck I'm talking about.

In 2008, I played a few games for Anstey Nomads, but only because I used to go and watch my brother turning out for them. They were at a decent standard in the Senior League Premier, and I'd be there turning up drunk to watch on from the sidelines. The manager used to ask me every time if I'd come and play for them – and I'd tell him no chance. Not because of my knees particularly, but because I just didn't want to play football. I didn't want to take anyone's spot, and I'd fallen out with the game by then.

But one day I turned up and he said, 'Listen, we haven't got any subs – I don't have a proper team.' He'd signed me on previously just in case I changed my mind, so I said yes. I borrowed some boots and played up front.

I didn't particularly enjoy the game – it was 1-1, late on, at a time when Anstey were going for the league. I've mentioned before that I'm at my best when someone tells me I can't do something – and the same thing happened here. The kid who was playing against me couldn't wait to have a pop.

'Premiership? You're fucking awful.'

I probably had been up to that point. But the next time I got the ball, I thought I'd try to show the little bastard. I got the ball and just ran, rolling back the years for 30 seconds before smashing one into the top corner. I walked over to him, half-cut, and grinned back, 'Listen, big man – why are you having a go at me? You don't even know my name.'

'Yes I do – you're Matt Piper.'

'That's funny, because I haven't got a fucking clue what your name is.'

He didn't have a comeback for that one.

I played a couple more games for Anstey after that, but even though I scored a few more goals, I didn't love it. I enjoyed the post-match drinking with the lads more.

Around this time, I'd also started doing some work for Leicester City, coaching their youngsters. One morning, I turned up at the stadium for an away game in Manchester, ready to go. All I'd have to do was sit there and be with the young lads, as it was well known – a running joke, even – that I wouldn't ever be able to drive the minibus on a Sunday morning. The other coaches knew I went out a lot, but they didn't realise the extent of it. I'd get out of bed, then get myself 'straight' by having a shower, popping chewing gums and spraying deodorant, turning up trying to look like I hadn't been steaming hours earlier.

But on this particular morning, one of the other coaches had come down ill.

'You're going to have to drive, Pipes.'

Fear. Panic. Utter dread. In the front of the bus was a physio; in the back, 15 kids ready to go. I wanted to sink into the ground. Obviously, I didn't want to drive and put all of those kids in danger; by the same token, I didn't want to admit to all of those other coaches that I was basically still drunk from the night before. It was one or the other, and in my head, both situations were awful. I'd done some bad things during this stage of my life – and on another day, this incident could have been added to the list.

But thank God the other side of my brain won out. It was the first moment I felt that I had to own up and admit my state. Jon Rudkin was Leicester's academy director back then, but I had to pull him aside. I broke down in tears. I knew I had to tell him that I might have a problem. There was no way I could drive.

Jon became Leicester's director of football in 2014, a massive job at the top of a football club going places, but right then he was unbelievable with me. It felt like half of him already knew I was going through a very difficult period in my life, and instead of having a go at me, he spoke to me on a level.

'Don't worry – but you're clearly not in a position to be working for the club right now,' he told me. 'Get yourself well and I'll give you a job again in the future.'

I got the arm-round-the-shoulder treatment: him telling me I was a great lad and couldn't let this drinking get the better of me. But it still didn't stop me. Jon had given me that unbelievable speech … but I carried on. It was one of the things that added to me getting help, but still wasn't *the* thing.

It sounds like madness when I talk about it now – breaking down in front of your boss, your brother calling you an embarrassment, your mum crying in your living room every day – but that's just the place I was in then.

In the end, it took something much worse for me to see light at the end of the tunnel.

All these things were happening in my life, and I was desperate to stop drinking. I'd say to myself, 'Right, this is the day.' On one day in particular, I remember thinking: I'm not going to drink today – I'm going to go for a run instead. By this point, I was about 17-and-a-half stone; in the Premiership I had been more like 11-and-a-half. I was huge, in a rut and desperate to change my lifestyle.

I live near a graveyard where my grandad was buried, so started running around it every day. I don't know why, but I would put on Eric Clapton's version of *Knockin' On Heaven's Door* while I did it – a great song, but not exactly the kind to bring you out of a bad place. If anything, it sends you deeper. I'd be there jogging, that song filling my ears, looking at all of these gravestones thinking, 'I just want to go home and drink.' That song took me to a place where death didn't feel very far away and I wasn't bothered. Life was fucked.

One day, I was at home, having not drunk for a day or two, my hands shaking from withdrawals, going on these runs and listening to that song. I thought: *today is the day. I'm going to get steaming.* So I went to the petrol station, grabbed some whisky and nailed two bottles in a few hours. On the kitchen worktop, there were all these pills of different brands; pots and blister packs, like an amateur pharmacy. I got everything out and there were still plenty of Valium tablets left. I hadn't smoked that day, but I was smashed. So, I got all of these pills out: sleeping tablets, paracetamol, co-codamol, codeine – everything, like Smarties all over the place. I grabbed handfuls and blasted them down with booze.

I don't remember having the thought in my head of, 'This is to kill myself' – but clearly, I didn't care whether I was doing that or not. There were times when my thought process was so blurred that I remember thinking my kids might be better off if I wasn't around. In the long term, they would have got the proceeds from my career: my house; my pension. It's how selfish you get, thinking that money will solve problems. I was thinking that money could be my way of helping them towards a better life.

I can say all of this today knowing that I'm about as far from that kind of dad as it's possible to be. Now I know that it doesn't matter if I can't buy them a house or give them all their first car – if I'm there for them, guiding the way as a responsible adult, I'm giving them much more than something monetary. What I live for now is being there with whatever my family needs: that comforting feeling of just knowing I'm around whenever they want me for support, a chat or anything else. It's trying to be that blend of my own mum and dad – protective, but loving. Any situation, anywhere, I'll be there for them.

But at that point in early 2009, my thought processes were just a dank smog. After all of these crazy episodes, this was the final act: 30 or 40 pills sliding down my throat.

I walked to the graveyard with a bottle of whisky in my hand. At the beginning, I remember having this really light-hearted, euphoric feeling as the drugs started to take over my body. Then I started to get a terrible stomach ache.

ENGLAND UNDER 21 INTERNATIONAL MATCH
REEBOK STADIUM, BOLTON WANDERERS F.C.
Friday 6th September 2002

ENGLAND V *YUGOSLAVIA*

KIRKLAND Chris	1	1	POLEKSIĆ Vukasin (C)
SAMUEL Jlloyd	2	2	NASTIĆ Nenad
KONCHESKY Paul	3	3	MIJAILOVIĆ Nikola
JENAS Jermaine	4	4	LOVRE Goran
BRAMBLE Titus	5	5	VIDIĆ Nemanja
BARRY Gareth (C)	6	6	JOKIĆ Djordje
PENNANT Jermaine	7	7	LAZOVIĆ Danko
CARRICK Michael	8	8	NOVKOVIĆ Srdjan
JEFFERS Francis	9	9	DELIBASIĆ Andrija
DEFOE Jermain	10	10	NOVAKOVIĆ Mitar
PRUTTON David	11	11	MATIĆ Igor
CLARKE Peter	12	12	DISLYENKOVIĆ Vladimir
HOWARTH Russell	13	13	KEKEZOVIĆ Dejan
PARNABY Stuart	14	14	JOKSIMOVIĆ Nebojsa
LESCOTT Joleon	15	15	PEKOVIĆ Mitar
AMEOBI Shola	16	16	BAKOVIĆ Branko
WRIGHT-PHILLIPS Shaun	17	17	JOVANOVIĆ Milan
CROUCH Peter	18	18	VUJOSEVIĆ Nikola
ETHERINGTON Matthew	19		
PIPER Matthew	20		
O'NEILL Gary	21		
EVANS Rhys	22		
TAYLOR Matt	23		

REFEREE:	Mr Kristinn Jakobsson
ASSISTANT:	Mr Pjetur Sigurdsson
ASSISTANT:	Mr Eyjolfur Finnsson
4TH OFFICIAL:	Mr Graham Laws

Sadly, I didn't win an official England Under-21 cap – but with that squad, you can see why. The opposition centre-back wasn't bad either...

FA Cup semi-final, 2004: I might have won this battle against Tim Cahill, but he – and Millwall – sadly won that war. Gutting.

'Hair today, top flight tomorrow,' read the dodgy newspaper headline. Sadly, both of those ambitions disappeared very shortly afterwards.

A barely recognisable 17-and-a-half stone on my first day at Sporting Chance. I was in a bad way at that point, but thankfully they helped to turn my life around.

I couldn't have done any of it without the help of my incredible mum and brother: two of my favourite people on the planet.

I'm so grateful to have my three brilliant boys: (left to right) Brandan, Finlay and Kairo. Being their dad makes me proud every single day.

Marrying my soulmate Leanne in August 2015, celebrating with the four wonderful kids we share between us.

At Rutland Water with Leanne, my step-daughter Sienna and sons Brandan, Finlay and Kairo. Our bicycle was made for two...

A very blessed man today: I'm much happier now than when I was a professional footballer.

I've been fortunate to meet my hero Gazza several times: as a player, in Sporting Chance and in my media work at Leicester. A lovely guy.

On the road with our hard-working Radio Leicester team – Ian Stringer (left), Owynn Palmer-Atkin (right) and honorary member: Kasabian's Tom Meighan (middle).

I'm so proud of our FSD Academy and the students within it. Here we are together at the King Power Stadium before a game against Brooke House.

And then the heart palpitations began.

I lay down on my grandad's grave. That's the last thing I can remember.

Into the black.

Knock, knock, knockin' on heaven's door …

It was my mum who found me.

She'd come to the house for her daily check, and I wasn't there. My phone was, my car was, my keys were. I don't know whether it was a mother's intuition or instinct, but she'd obviously scouted the house for me and knew I'd started running a bit by this point.

Mum went straight to my grandad's grave – her dad's – and found me laying on it. Somehow, she managed to get me into her car as I was slipping in and out of consciousness. She was crying.

'Oh God. Oh God, you silly boy. What have you done?'

But I couldn't talk. Eventually, we got to the hospital, where they pumped my stomach and tried to get me stable. They got me to drink charcoal – it's often used in drug overdoses to help the body get rid of toxins. I wasn't awake when the doctors were discussing the possibility of sectioning me. I remember the guy's face afterwards, though, and saw that it could be serious. I didn't even know what being sectioned meant, but my mum's reaction had told me it was something bad – she'd got quite emotional with them to keep me out of that situation.

My mum is an unbelievable woman, and I don't know where I'd be without her. She never, ever gave up on me. She was there even when I didn't want her to be, and there when I needed her in the most desperate situation of my life. I put her through absolute hell – yet still, there she was by my side every step of the way. There's no other way to say it: her love saved my life.

And she kept me away from being sectioned. When she has to be, my mum is an absolute chat-shit champion – and I mean that in the most endearing way I can think of. When I was 14 years old, I was leaving my school in Anstey and the school all of my mates were going to was in Quorn, eight miles up the road. I was in the catchment area for three other schools – Beaumont Leys, Babington and John Ellis – but she didn't like any of them; she didn't really want me being around the inner-city boys of Leicester all day, every day. Quorn said no to taking me, though, so Mum had to attend a tribunal at County Hall. She isn't the most confident of public speakers in front of a large audience, but went there to fight my case. Afterwards, she told me that her voice had wobbled all the way through it. But she got me into that school.

A few weeks after my hospital visit, it suddenly dawned on me what she'd been through to do all of that for me. And finally, she got me the help I needed at Sporting Chance.

I feel shame now – a lot of it. I've met alcoholics since and seen it from the other side. Having been in their position myself, though, I know how things can fall on deaf ears. As I explained earlier, that pathway to getting help is a process rather than something that just happens straight away. You could have the most amazing person in front of you saying all the right things, but still not quite feel ready to ask the big question.

It was like that for me, too – it took a near-death experience, the thought of my boys growing up without their dad and the support of my amazing mum to pull me through to the other side.

But I was finally ready.

CHAPTER 18

A sporting chance

WHEN I came out of the Leicester Royal Infirmary, I saw a counsellor who more or less sent me away with a card and said, 'If you get into any more trouble, ring this number.'

She was very good and very nice, but I thought I'd be alright; that I'd sort myself out. I continued running at the graveyard behind my house and started to get fit in the next two or three weeks.

But I was still drinking. Not as much, but still drinking. It was better than before, though – I was starting to lose a bit of weight and feel a little better about myself. Suddenly, it all came back to me; finding cards from counsellors and other people who have been pushed your way in the past. Friends and family who'd reached out to help in the best way they could, telling me of cousins who'd been through something similar, and recommending experts who'd been really helpful to people they knew.

Back then, I'd sit there thinking, 'Do I ring these, or do I just get steaming?' It was one or the other, very black and white. It takes a lot of courage to make that first phone call, and back then, I didn't have it.

It all kicked off again: my brother was angry because he thought that I'd turned a corner; my mum was going through the same experiences. Dad had started talking to me again before that, but couldn't deal with it when I resumed. My mates weren't going on nights out with me, so I was just sitting in my house drinking. Alone, again.

It was also around the time that my third-born, Kairo, came along in March 2009 – and finally helped lead me to the right decision. Mum had been coming round every day before the incident, but she was there even more after that. I was still doing some of the same things, living in my own world, but I'd stopped gambling and become very reclusive after the hospital. I didn't want to see anyone. I'd be hiding from neighbours when I pulled up on my front – if they were walking by with their dog, I'd wait in my car pretending that I was on my phone until they went past so I didn't have to speak to them. That fear was very real.

Finally, I was at a point where I was ashamed of myself – and I knew that I had to get myself straight for my kids.

Thankfully, this tired old routine only lasted a few weeks after I'd got out. Mum came round one day, like any other. She was crying, begging – trying to relay the message that this wasn't me, that my path in life wasn't destined to carry on this way. There had to be something more out there for me. That was always her message.

She said she'd been told of this place called Sporting Chance. After everything, the penny finally dropped: maybe I *should* listen to her after all.

I didn't know anything about Sporting Chance up to that point, but she mentioned Tony Adams and it resonated with me – my old man had been a huge Arsenal fan, and up until I was about 14, I was still supporting them alongside Leicester. If they played each other, I'd want it to be a draw. Adams' name was powerful in our house when I was growing up – my dad used to talk of him in high esteem as the club's captain. She knew that too. I also knew that Paul Merson and Lee Dixon were patrons, the former having dealt with his own demons in the past.

Finally, that clear thought emerged: let's drive down and give this thing a try. Mum had already spoken to them and got me a spot. Now all I had to do was stay clean and sober for 24 hours.

Sporting Chance is based at a Champneys resort in Hampshire within an amazing wooded area – it's unbelievable. As I saw what looked like a cottage on the approach there, I remember thinking to myself that it felt like being in a children's fairy-tale. You drive through these woods, which open out to a clearing with its accommodation in the middle. It was beautiful.

Adams had set up the charity in 2000 with £165,000 of his own money, enlisting the help of Elton John to be an early patron and gradually building up something very special over time. His old therapist, James West, became his clinical director, while his good friend Peter Kay – a fellow former addict who he'd met in AA – took over as CEO. James and Peter would both become very familiar to me soon enough. The latter had once been in a coma for 21 days, suffering kidney failure and a cardiac arrest, before getting out of hospital and continuing to drink. As Adams later explained, that kind of behaviour makes sense when you're an addict. I was proof of it. Eventually, though, Peter – like Tony and James – had got sober and helped countless people to transform their lives. After Adams had eventually convinced the PFA to get on board with funding, Sporting Chance had everything it needed to succeed.

This was my big chance.

I drank on the way down, though, trying to hide the contents of my little plastic bottle from my mum in the car. It's hard to explain why someone would do that when they're on their way to getting proper help – I know it's even harder to understand. Some of it was the fear of failure, the thought of letting people down again. I always tried to protect myself by saying things like, 'If I don't like it, mum, I'm not staying.' The simple fact of it, though, was that I was just dependent.

Sporting Chance turned me away on that first day – they could tell I still had drink in my system, and said that I'd have to spend the night at a local hotel and then come back the next day. You *have* to want it. My mum was quite fearful at that point, understandably, but talked me into stopping at the hotel. There was definitely a part of me that thought, 'fuck this' and wanted to throw in the towel.

That was the easy way out. But I go back to her again, and the things she said: it had taken us a few hours to get there, we were down now so might as well stay the night, and I wouldn't drink because she was there. And I didn't – because I had Valium. That's the honest truth. I could go without a drink, so long as I had those pills with me.

When we had initially walked in on that first visit, though, we were greeted on the front desk and encouraged to go into a little side room to make a cup of tea while we waited to speak with somebody.

'This is Paul,' one of the younger counsellors, Chris, said to me.

'Nice to meet you, Paul,' I said to a bloke at the kettle.

He had his back to me then, but when he turned around I realised that 'Paul' wasn't just anyone – it was Gazza. At Sporting Chance, you can always just drop back whenever you like, and this just happened to be a day that he was returning to have a chat with everyone.

Growing up, Paul Gascoigne had been an absolute icon to me alongside Diego Maradona and Ian Wright. I went a bit fan boy on him for a while, and he was brilliant.

'Let's have a cup of tea together,' he said, then made me one.

We were only together for five minutes or so, but it felt like we had a lot in common. By this point I think Gascoigne was a few months sober, and told me he sympathised with my situation; that he knew how tough it was when you come out of football, especially so early. We'd both just been street footballers who played for the love of it – me in Leicester, him in Gateshead; working-class backgrounds where your mum and dad were trying to do everything they could for you. If you got a football at Christmas, that was happiness.

I try to relay these stories now to my kids. I'm not rich at all, but we provide them with a very comfortable life; they're never found wanting for anything. Sometimes, you look around at Christmas and wonder if you're spoiling them. My parents always looked out for me, but my upbringing was nothing like that. When two men are sitting there at rock bottom, you have that conversation and feel the vibes that you're quite similar. You both love the game but have turned your back on it for one reason or another, and haven't been able to deal with that. I'm sure Gazza won't remember our conversation now, but it was a very special five minutes in my life.

That was my first experience of life at Sporting Chance, and another reason why I stuck it out and went back to them the next day.

After meeting Gazza, I had a consultation with James – Adams' valued therapist with a crazy story of his own. He told me that he was a former gangster who rolled with the Adams family in London, knew the Krays and had been on his path to sobriety with Eric Clapton. He was also an incredibly inspiring guy: James had been over 20 years sober by that point, having previously been a heroin user.

'I used to be a fucking animal, Matt,' I remember him saying to me, with his thick cockney accent.

That's how he'd talk to you – straight up. As he was dropping all of these stories, I couldn't help but think, *'Jesus …'* I was sitting here with underworld royalty, essentially. If James could come through all of that and make it through the other side, then so could I.

I wasn't completely truthful with him, though. James asked me if I took any other drugs. I told him that I'd smoked a bit of weed, but not in the last 24 hours. I didn't tell him about the Valium, though – and that's what got me through that night in the hotel.

When I turned up the next day, I had an appointment with the doctor. He was a lovely bloke who you could chat to easily, and told me that the facility was taking me in – this was day one. But I had to be 100% truthful with him.

'Anything else you're addicted to – even if it's chocolate
– we want to know. Everything.'

This time, I didn't lie.

'How much do you take?'

When I told him it was 80mg every day, this experienced
doctor of years in the job nearly fell off his chair. That's
when it scared me. He told me that taking Valium in that
amount could damage organs – my liver, heart – and cause
serious harm. I begged him not to take it away from me,
though – and he didn't completely. Instead, for a couple of
weeks he put me on a reduction programme. On the first
day I took 70mg, the next day, 65mg … and on it went.
They didn't let me have sugar in my tea. I didn't have any
chocolate or sweets. All the Valium I had was locked away
by the doctor, and each morning I'd have to go down and
get that day's dosage from him. He'd count out the pills,
snap some in half and I'd always try it on with him.

'Don't bother snapping that one in half, doc – I'll just
have it.'

He didn't bend, though, and his doses were coming
down all the time – slowly, he was weaning me off it. After
15 days, I was clear of that drug. No drink. No chocolate.
No sugar. Nothing.

I didn't find going without alcohol too bad, in truth – it
was the Valium I was really fearful of losing. Before I went
into Sporting Chance, I'd always felt like if I had that, I'd
be OK. I had some withdrawals – a few panic attacks in

the middle of the night, where I'd wake up sweating with my heart pounding through my chest at a hundred miles an hour. There were days in rehab when I desperately wanted those tablets, but the thought of my boys at home always gave me the strength to carry on.

I told the doctor about my symptoms, and he was cool about it – he never let me up my dosage, but on some days it might just stay the same. The more that he spoke to me and gave me the facts, though, the more I understood what it was doing – or more accurately, had already done – to my body. They ran some tests and found that my liver function was not good at all; there was irreparable damage. If I carried on taking Valium, it would only get worse. The doctor gave me the facts, but did it in a way that was straightforward and not sugar-coated. I respected that, and his words started to hit home.

On my first 'true' day, there were three other starters – all ex-footballers in some capacity. There was an older guy who was in his 60s and a legend of Welsh football; a Northern Irish kid in his early 20s who'd finished at 18 without a contract and turned to drink and cocaine; then a lad from Manchester who'd been a party animal, popping pills all the time after not making a first-team appearance at his Lancashire club. Because they'd all signed professional contracts, they were all entitled to that help from the PFA. There were two rooms there, so three of us shared and let our elder new friend have his own.

You're all in there for the same reasons, so you become quite close.

As I started to wean off the drugs, I began smoking cigarettes again to 'replace' them. But they were fine with that – it helps to keep a little vice in your life when you've just lost everything else. Even though smoking is very detrimental to your health, it's not getting steaming every day, hoovering Valium like sweets and getting high all the time. From what I can remember, all of the therapists smoked, so I'd often be outside with them in the garden building my relationships with them even further.

The first thing that's liberating about Sporting Chance is that you're surrounded by all of these positive people who don't drink or take drugs – it's uplifting. The way they talk is articulate and sharp. They're clever people who know what they're doing. It's the *cool* thing to not do those things. When you go into any new environment, you look up to the top for your role models – they're who you want to be like. That's why that place is so special.

Chris introduced me to a guy called Julian, who ended up becoming my main counsellor. He was unbelievable – a listener who would just encourage you to dump everything on him from your mind. Then he'd just say something wise at the end to sum it all up. Sometimes, he'd kill it with something really simple that got through to you.

'You're human – you've made some mistakes, but it's not that bad and not too late. You're a good person.'

These counsellors would do two or three days per week at Sporting Chance, then run their own private practices in London. They'd never reveal who else they were helping at that time, but I know there were some huge celebrities among their clients – ex-footballers, catwalk models, actors.

There was never anything too deep about my chats with Julian. What helped me most from the start was knowing that I wasn't the only one who was feeling like this. When you're sitting at home, drinking and smoking, thinking you're the worst person in the world with all of these problems, you look around and don't see everyone else dealing with the same things. In rehab, though, it's the opposite – you're more like the majority than the few. It flips everything on its head.

The four therapists took turns to do sleepovers with us. There was also Peter Kay, who was the loveliest bloke you could imagine – a great eccentric who would come in with purple trousers and yellow socks, and who sadly passed away in 2013. Each therapist had been an addict in the past and had their own distinct styles. I appreciated James's approach.

'Come in here and tell me all your fears and the horrible things you've done,' he'd say.

So you'd tell him about how you manipulated and mistreated people.

'Yeah, that's pretty fucking horrible, Matt. I'll tell you what I used to do …'

Then James would recall his own stories, some of which I found quite shocking. But in Sporting Chance they are very good at helping you to rationalise your thoughts and actions. You can go to some dark places when you're in a depressed state, but James told me one thing that has always stuck with me since: 'I am human, so nothing is alien to me.'

You are not alone.

Eventually, we were introduced to Alcoholics Anonymous.

At the start, you're terrified. You go to meetings around the local area; sometimes driving five minutes, sometimes half an hour. You see all of these people telling different stories about themselves: one guy said he used to pour vodka into his car's windscreen wash container, so he could just take a straw into his garage and drink straight from it. If his wife came in, it would just look like he was working on his car. There were some crazy tales.

The first time we went to AA, it was with James. He told our group that we didn't have to share – but that he would, and we could if we wanted to. I knew from the moment I sat down in that first meeting, it wasn't going to happen then. There was a look between us all that said: *not a chance.*

You're sitting there hearing all of these mad, amazing stories, and then James steps in. He told us about Eric Clapton, who was in sobriety when he heard the news that his four-year-old son had died after falling out of a Manhattan apartment window in 1991. Hours later, he didn't go back to heroin, cocaine or alcohol – he was in an AA meeting. Clapton made it through the whole of that horrendous period in his life without relapsing.

'That's how powerful these meetings are,' he said.

It gave me goosebumps. James told that story to everyone in the room, but I think he did it to send a powerful message to the four of us in particular; the power of AA, and what sharing can do.

I shared in my second AA meeting. We were with Julian this time, and because he was my therapist, he told me that it would be nice if I said something. I told him I didn't know what to put out there.

'Just tell them your story,' he said.

It's the sort of scenario where you just have to get in if you want to speak – there's no formal process or queue; you just go for it when the moment comes. I went to speak three or four times before the moment finally came, but Julian just gave me a look that said I'd get my chance eventually. And I did.

'Hi, I'm Matt – and I'm an alcoholic.'

'Hi, Matt.'

By then, though, I'd built up to speaking so much that my mind went blank. What was I going to say now?

I can't remember exactly what came out, but it was only a brief introduction about my story. I specifically didn't say that I used to be a footballer, but told them that what I used to love doing had come to an end and I found that very difficult. I'd started drinking, taking drugs and was trying to get through it. Detail was lacking – it was short, messy and not very sweet.

Before you leave Sporting Chance, you have to have gone through all of the 12 steps of AA. Traditionally, they're steeped in religion, but I remember James telling me that you just had to read them in a certain way. To believe in the 12-step programme, you first have to accept that you are not the highest power on Earth.

The step that I remember most was the one about trying to make amends for what I'd done. If I felt like I'd ever been out of order with someone, or hurt people, then I had to engage with them again and at least try to apologise. I remember making my list of people, but some I just couldn't even remember; all of those random, blank faces on drunken days and nights. I wanted to apologise for every little mistake I'd ever made, and was horrified by the idea of hurting or being rude to anyone in the slightest of ways. But most importantly, I wanted to make things right with my family and become the dad I knew I could be.

They introduced football on the sixth or seventh day with a guy called Jon Goodman, a former player who later joined the Nike Academy and worked for clubs including Leeds and Tottenham. He'd just do simple games with us like footgolf, where we'd be booting a ball around the grounds aiming at trees. But something as simple as that made me fall back in love with the game. I looked at Jon and thought: *that's what I want to do*. I've met him since over the years, and try to portray how much of an effect those sessions of his had on me. He was an A-licence coach, so doing a bit of footgolf was basically a school session to him, but it just took me back to a time when I loved the game; there was no pressure, and you were just having fun. Whether he designed those sessions to make that happen I don't know, but it worked. When I've spoken to him since, he didn't seem like he believed me – but it's true.

Jon would talk to me quite deeply about coaching and next steps. At that point, I had my Level 2 qualification and he told me that I should go for my UEFA badge, and said I'd make a good coach at some point – I could communicate well and had played at a high level. He instilled a lot of confidence in me that way. At that moment, I decided that I either wanted to become a football coach or a counsellor. Those thoughts were the first shoots springing from the earth of owning my own academy and trying to shape youngsters' lives for the better.

Another thing Sporting Chance encouraged was using the gym more. I lost three stone in four weeks – and that was where the ego kicked in. The girls at Champneys started looking at me in a way that I remember they once did when I was a footballer or growing up; I'd lost a lot of weight in my face, my body was returning to a more normal size, and I just looked fitter overall. Even the colour of my skin was healthier.

Looking in the mirror started becoming less of an ordeal. You see progress, and it feels good. I had a big beard when I went in, and it looked awful. But I remember waking up one day, feeling happy because I'd lost some weight, and decided to have a shave. I borrowed one of the lads' clippers and got rid of the face fuzz, so I was clean shaven.

'Fucking hell, Pipes, you look like Ruud Gullit!' one of the lads said.

I'll never forget that – mainly because I have never, ever looked like Ruud Gullit. But it was funny. As I kept going, I reached a point where I decided that I was going to look after myself, and I've carried that love of health and fitness with me ever since.

There was one more type of therapy that Sporting Chance swore by: equine. I couldn't understand it: how was a horse supposed to stop me from drinking?

The horse sanctuary, as it turned out, was run by actress Kika Mirylees – she used to be in *Bad Girls* in the early noughties, as one of the air-headed trolley dollies. I recognised her straight away, but was far more used to seeing her as that swearing rebel on TV. Obviously, Kika was absolutely nothing like that in real life.

'Yes, my darling – I was in that show,' she said to me. 'Did you like it?'

We visited the sanctuary two or three times per week, for the full six weeks, and got our own horse to look after: brushing them, helping to clean their hooves, taking them for walks. You don't ride them, because they're all horses that had been abused in the past. Mine was from Portugal and called Marron: he was beautiful, big and strong, but had lash marks all over his body where he'd been beaten in the past. It was horrible: these deep scars from where he'd been whipped to the flesh.

A horse doesn't stop you from drinking – but it's hard to overstate how effective therapy like that can be. They almost mirror human beings' moods – it's said that they have a sixth sense for that kind of thing. At first, it was hard. Having abused myself and been the kind of selfish character I was, closed to the world and sending out negative vibes, I wasn't getting very far with Marron. For days, I'd go up to him: he'd be looking at me, I'd be looking at him, and then suddenly he'd just bolt off. I would try to go near him again, he'd give me a sniff, then run away once more.

But gradually, over time, he became my new best mate – Marron would do anything I wanted to. Kika taught us commands and I soon became much closer with him. As I fed, groomed and did all of these things with him, I began to realise that he had been abused like I was abusing myself. There was some kind of deeper connection there; it didn't matter that he was a horse and I was a human. Kika was trying to send us the message that if you pushed out more positivity in your life, then better things would come your way.

All of the lads I was with were in agreement – it was our favourite thing to do at Sporting Chance. We did AA, yoga, meditation, counselling and more, but the two things I loved to do most were playing football and seeing Marron.

That relationship with him helped me in later life, without question. Think about it in terms of kids. They don't lie to you. If they get a bad vibe around someone, they're not coming anywhere near. A horse is very similar: if they don't like you, they won't engage. That time with Marron definitely helped me heal.

I don't want to say that I'd be dead without Sporting Chance, because I just don't know. But without doubt, it was an incredibly important period in my life for becoming the person I am now. If I'd continued the way I was going, then realistically I wouldn't have been on this planet for much longer.

Sporting Chance allowed me to understand myself and my thought processes, and how to think about both on a different level. I didn't have those tools before. I was seriously struggling – it wasn't just being in a depressed state, but also having no idea of how to get out of it and deal with that adversity.

Most importantly, it helped to give me the focus that would change my life – and I'll forever be grateful for that.

CHAPTER 19

Away goes trouble
down the drain

THE HARDEST part of rehab is coming out of that
environment and going back to your normal life.

You're not the same character who left: the life and soul
of every party who got fucked up and did crazy stuff all
the time. You're not that guy anymore. People can't believe
you don't drink – all of a sudden you're the dunce of every
room, not the entertainer.

But when I got out of Sporting Chance, I was excited
about a new beginning. A new start. Someone I'd been
hanging around with in the old days told me that I had
a new kind of arrogance about me, that because I wasn't
drinking, I thought I was superior to other people.

I batted that away, but then sat and thought about it
for a few days. They may have said it in the wrong way,
but they were also right to an extent. I wasn't drinking

278

any more, I was clean, I had crystal-clear thoughts – I was moving on to the next stage.

It wasn't that I was better than anyone else, but I felt like Sporting Chance had opened my eyes to a different kind of world. It's a very powerful feeling: when you come out of there, you feel like you're on a different path to everyone else. It doesn't come from a big-headed place – I just felt like I had learned a lot about myself and the previous life I was living. I felt like I'd grown so much, even though I was only in there for six weeks.

The only fear I had initially was around my mates. I'd want to see them, they'd want to see me – but what kind of situation was that going to be in? Normally, when I saw them it was at the pub, on a night out, for a meal – always surrounded by drink. I thought it would be tough.

I think there were feelings from certain people at the start: don't invite this guy out, because he's going to ruin everyone's night with his sobriety. I was never a mood-killer when I wasn't drinking, though, and never asked people not to do it around me. But it was difficult. Bank holidays were hardest, being around people who were steaming while remembering how much I used to look forward to those weekends. The mates who'd kept me at a distance during my worst moments and didn't want to indulge my habits were brilliant, though, and all came back into my life – sometimes even saying we'd go out together and not drink. But I didn't want that.

You start again with your relationships, desperate to distance yourself from some of the behaviours you demonstrated before. Some of the people I'm close to now were actually ones I met when I was steaming all the time. I had to get to know those people again, and I'm not going to lie – sometimes it was really awkward. Importantly, though, I had to make amends to those I was closest with. I found it very helpful, and thankfully, my family and good friends accepted my apologies. They could see I meant it, and that I was trying.

On the first day I got out of Sporting Chance, I went to visit my nan at the hospital – she had vascular dementia, and had been struggling to recognise family members for a few months. She had 14 grandchildren, but Dan and I were really close to her because we saw my mum's parents so often. She'd played a massive part in shaping us when we were growing up. It was late in the evening for my visit, and the nurses had let me stay a little longer than the allocated hours, as they knew I'd been away for a while. When I said goodbye to her that night, I turned back to give her another hug, tell her that I loved her and that I would see her again soon.

'I love you too, Matt,' she said back. And then again.

I rang my mum straight away in shock to tell her what had happened.

That night, my nan passed away. It was like she'd waited for me to come out of rehab before she could go on with her journey. I still miss her every single day.

A couple of months after I got out, my best mate was getting married. Beforehand, I felt so confident that everything would be fine – I knew loads of people there. I would have been one of his best men, but told him that I couldn't do that so soon after coming out of rehab. Otherwise, I didn't feel any apprehension about it.

When I got into the venue, though, it all changed. I *needed* a drink. I just didn't feel confident in that social environment when everyone else was steaming, and people were coming up to me with the same question.

'Oh my God, don't you drink anymore? *Really?*'

I felt anxious and left to clear my head for a while. I walked down the road to a Tesco and bought a bottle of white wine – who knows why, as I never used to drink it. I sat in a derelict car park, opened the bottle and sat staring at it for about an hour. In the end, I poured it away and went back to the party.

When I went into the room again, there was a bloke in the corner, slightly tipsy, who came up to me.

'Mate, me and my missus have been watching you since you came in – how well dressed and handsome a fella you are.'

I'm not making this up, I promise. I thanked him for his nice words, but told him if he knew what had just happened, he wouldn't have all of that praise for me. We got chatting and I told him the story: the car park, rehab. He said it helped him, and that he had those kinds of tendencies and struggles too. Hearing that someone else was in the same boat made him feel better. He called his wife over. It was like a counselling meeting – but it was positive for me in that situation as well. It made me feel good that I'd helped another person by sharing my story with them.

I kept seeing Julian for two years or so after I came out – paid for by the PFA once a month for the first year, and then I carried it on myself because I felt like I needed a bit more support. It started off once a week in Fulham – I'd get on the train and go down. I'd just talk to him about anything that was going on in my life at that point, and could ring him any time I wanted to. I often did that for the first few weeks, two or three times per day. You end up missing the counsellors who essentially became your heroes in that place.

'... and how did that make you feel?'

Well, Julian, I wanted to punch the guy.

'Did you really? People have thoughts all the time – it doesn't mean that defines them as a person, or you have to act on them.'

There was a lot of growing up in those meetings; not just with Julian and I, either. When you're a footballer and go through the system, you're in a bubble. As a young player, having everything done for you, you don't always get that time to grow up as a young adult. There's a lot of general shit in day-to-day life that people in that kind of environment just don't understand straight away.

I was still going to AA meetings three times per week in Leicester, too. The more you go to them, the more confident you get. Talking in public had always been one of my biggest fears – at school, if I knew in advance that I had to read out a portion of *Romeo & Juliet* in class, I'd get the most convenient stomach ache to get me out of doing it. Whatever it took. But in AA, you have to get over that fear – and I honestly believe it ended up helping me in later life with public speaking and being on the radio regularly.

I didn't know exactly what I wanted to do with my life at this point, but I'd identified wanting to be someone who helped other people develop. In Sporting Chance, you're surrounded by counsellors who do that all day long, and it's inspiring. You've also got the yoga teachers and the likes of Jon and Kika – all of them trying to help develop you as a person.

At some point, I thought that I wanted to be a counsellor; I actually enrolled on a course, and Julian was trying to help me start that process. Ultimately, though, I just decided that I wasn't ready for that – the idea that in three years' time, I could be on the other side of a table hearing people saying the same stuff that I'd been saying only months earlier. I didn't feel like I'd be capable of dealing with that back then.

I still had a mortgage on my house, but as soon as I came out, my thoughts were far more sensible. I was drinking before because my money was running out and I didn't know what I was doing, but as soon as you start to think more logically, everything begins to change. I had a pension, I had some assets, I had a couple of houses – financially, it wasn't a complete disaster. In my dark days, I was wondering how I could continue my way of life for another year or two – there was no structure there, so I'd just blow it all. I'd sell off something big, do nothing, not try to get a job and then spend money like it was water.

After rehab, though, I began to plan things properly and manage what I had, selling off the odd thing to help cover other bits like gaining coaching badges. I also started planning something called Pro Transition. Within a week of getting into Sporting Chance, I'd had the idea. How can a guy – not just me, but so many others – finish something like professional football, and then the next help he gets is when he's trying to kill himself? I'm not saying I would have been open to the PFA's help when I retired, but money alone didn't help me – there was no proactive action to support the process.

Setting up Pro Transition kept me driven for six months when I got out – I had marketing done, business cards made, and wrote up the programme of a support structure I thought was needed when a player came out of the game. It could be for anyone – from young lads who'd been let go, to players like me who'd finished early through injury, all the way through to those who'd had full careers and finished naturally.

Pro Transition was about counselling, physiotherapy, exercise, fitness, job recruitment – everything. I wanted a portal where players could uploaded their profiles, and then we'd create a bespoke package to help them reach the next stage of their lives with PFA help. We would encourage players to speak with each other, sharing ideas and getting support from others in a similar situation. It felt like a really good thing.

I'd had some very promising initial discussions with the PFA. It had passed a couple of hurdles of people who said they really liked the idea, and I was told that it sounded like the kind of thing they might be interested in getting behind. Then, suddenly, it was all over before it had got off the ground. Martin Buchan, a former Manchester United player in the '70s and '80s who later joined the PFA, absolutely shot it to bits.

We had a phone meeting, before which I'd got all the encouragement I needed to suggest that it would get Pro Transition up and running. But Buchan ripped it to shreds.

'People get in contact with us all the time with ideas like this, and then we end up funding it all,' he told me. 'You haven't put any financial commitments into it yourself, or got other backers, so for us it's a no-go.'

I was devastated. Not to the point where I wanted to pick up a bottle, but I was living in this new world thinking, 'This is going to help a lot of people.' It felt real to me, and annoys me a little now because there are a lot of similar companies out there now doing very well – backed by the PFA, too.

Luckily, by this point I did at least have other things to keep my mind busy. Jon Rudkin had stayed true to his word and offered me a coaching job at Leicester City, very soon after I'd got out.

'Any way we can help you, Pipes – we want you to come back to the football club.'

It was brilliant of him. He got in touch with me first to ask how I was, and said he'd heard that I'd gone through rehab and stopped drinking. Then he offered me a role as a mentor to the under-18s, and a coach with the under-15s.

At this point, I also met Dale Bradshaw, who was the club's academy welfare officer back then. She would just sit there and listen to me where not many others had done that before, and through that period – even to this day, actually – Dale was a huge help in my life: the perfect person for me to meet at that time.

One of the big things I thought when I came out of Sporting Chance was that if anyone asked me to do anything positive from then on, I'd say yes to it – see where it took me. Leicester put me on a retainer contract, and I was also travelling to away games with the youth team manager, Steve Beaglehole. I loved it, and it gave me something to focus on a few times per week, writing up sessions and planning the next ones.

That said, the money was shocking – people are willing to do that job for free. And mine was starting to run out. There was only so much longer I could rely on my assets to get me through, so I really needed something that would give me some long-term stability.

Leicester did enrol me on a course to get my Level 3 (UEFA B) coaching badge, though. Muzzy Izzet was also doing a bit of coaching there at the time, and as it turned out, the club had put him on the same course. When we were players at Leicester, Muzzy was an absolute legend – I was just a little whipper-snapper trying to get into the team. You might like each other's personalities, but you're never going to be best mates because that's just the way things are when up-and-comers are going into an elite environment. He was a cracking lad during our days at Filbert Street, but that relationship was never anything more than respectful and fleeting.

At that point, I still looked up to him like I did when I was a kid at Leicester – even though I was an older man by then and long finished in football. He was the hero and I was the apprentice. But before we got started, the club got in contact.

'Muzzy would like your number – is that alright?'

He called me up and suggested we lift-share to St George's Park, so we ended up spending a lot of time together. On those car journeys to Burton, I told him my story about the things that had happened to me since I left Leicester. He didn't know any of it, like a lot of people in football – to him, I'd just come in, done well, got sold to Sunderland and then struggled with injuries. Done. Suddenly, I was like Lenny Henry to him as I recalled all of the madness that had happened since then – he couldn't believe it.

Muzzy and I were the only former players on the course, but we'd socialise with all of the lads on it every Friday and have a brilliant time. I look back fondly on those days getting to know Muz so well – we had such a laugh, and became close. He came to my wedding, years later, and I'll always remember the message he wrote in our guest book.

'Well who knew it? We played together at the same club for so many years without really knowing each other, then went on our Level 3 and became close friends. I've never enjoyed three months of my life as much as on that course.'

When I was setting up the FSD Academy later on, we would have theoretically become a rival to Muzzy's own academy in Leicestershire. But he gave me hours and hours on the phone every week for six months to support me and help get us set up. That's just the kind of lad he is.

Thankfully, those good times were a sign of things to come – even if the crazy stories weren't quite over just yet.

CHAPTER 20

Into the light

I HAVEN'T yet spoken much about my wife Leanne in this book, but I need to: we've been very happily married since August 2015, and every single day I count my lucky stars that we're together.

True to the rest of my story, though, meeting her in the first place wasn't exactly straightforward. At the time, I was doing a personal training course with a guy – let's call him Liam – who I'd known for a few years. When I first met him as a teenager, I was in Pilot buying clothes; it was a time before I'd got into Leicester's first team or anywhere close, but when people had started to hear of my name from performances in the reserves. Liam walked into the shop … and he was *huge*. He was the same age as me, but made me look like a little boy. I'd also heard stories about him, knocking bouncers out on wild nights, but also rising up as an aspiring boxer in the ring, undefeated so far in his amateur career. He was thinking of turning pro. So although we had very different lifestyles at that time, our lives were aligned in some ways. We got chatting.

'I'm out this weekend, mate – why don't you come with us?' he asked me.

So I did. It was strange being out with Liam, because people would be giving you a wide berth. Normally, I'd have been chirpily talking to different people, but with him there was a different feeling. People nodded at you, but there was fear. Still, I continued to hang around with him at that time and we stayed friendly throughout my football career.

Liam did turn pro as a boxer in the end, winning his first four fights but then losing the fifth to a lucky body shot. It killed his confidence, and he quit soon after that – but not for bright new things. Instead, he became a bit of a gangster: he knew he was a tough kid from a tough, single-parent upbringing, and thought he could use his skills to earn some good money on the street. We stayed in touch, but not particularly closely.

I had money when I finished football, but even more time on my hands. So I decided to hit the gym – not because I was particularly desperate to get buff or fit back then, but because it was one of the only things to do in the daytime. As it turned out, Liam went to the same gym, and we reconnected there. A lot of my nights out were with him, and he became a very close friend over that time.

But it almost took me down another road entirely. One day, he asked me to step into his world. I always believe he did it from a good place, though, because he knew I was struggling for money at the time.

'Listen,' he said. 'I've got a job, quite an easy one, and I'd like you to come in on it with me – because I need someone I trust 100%.'

In short, his acquaintances had got information about a dealer from another city who was coming into town. He was staying in a hotel, and would have either drugs or money with him. This dealer was also going on a night out – and would leave it all behind in his room while he was gone. All my mate wanted me to do was sit in the car park and keep watch for if the dealer came back.

'It's easy – you're not in harm's way. There's £10,000 in it for you.'

I said I'd let him know later that day – and looking back to the place I was in, I'm very proud that I turned him down. It might have been easy work, but it felt like if I'd stepped into that world even for a while, I was in it for good. But his reaction was another reason why I liked him. This was a guy who wanted someone he trusted to do a job for him – and in that industry, people tend to get their way.

'Cool, brother – I just thought I'd ask you. It's no problem.'

I saw him a couple of days later, £80,000 richer.

When I came out of Sporting Chance in May 2009, I did so with the absolute intention of never drinking again. I'd had the shakes without booze in there, but they were only because my body had gotten so used to whisky and I'd deprived it of that for weeks on end.

For the most part, though, whenever I had to say the words, 'Hi, I'm Matt … and I'm an alcoholic', it was never with the greatest conviction.

Let me stress now: that can be a very dangerous thing to think for a lot of alcoholics – so many go into AA feeling that way, when in fact they are very dependent on the booze. I *was* an alcoholic at that stage of my life.

When things were bad, I used drink to get through a very difficult time. I need focus in my life and booze was exactly that for me, back then. If I was going to drink, then I was going to be dedicated to the art of drinking – even if it was Bell's Whisky. I had nothing else going for me.

I went a year without touching a drop of alcohol again, but by that time, things were completely different. I was back in a very good place, things were looking up financially, and everything felt settled. My thoughts were clear – nothing felt crazy any more. Fast-forward a few years, and Liam and I were on a PT course together – both having drastically changed our lives, and looking ahead to something new. We were going out together again, and he had become a good friend. Whereas some other people had been forcing the drink issue a bit, he never did – he just knew I didn't, so left me alone. But we'd go out and have a good time.

At the same time, I remember driving up to Nottingham with him and Stevo for a PT course one day, telling them I felt ready to settle down with someone. I just hadn't met anyone I liked yet.

'I know a girl I think you'd get on with,' Liam told me.

From Monday to Friday for three weeks, we were doing this intense course, driving there every morning together and then driving back later on. Basically, we were spending a lot of time together – so he gave me her number. That night, I called Leanne up and we chatted for hours – it just felt so easy. It was one of those calls where you've been on the phone for four hours with no idea of where the time has gone. I said to her, 'I'm going out in a couple of weeks – it would be great to see you out.' She agreed.

On the night, Liam and I decided to treat ourselves to a hotel room at the Hilton – he was drinking in the hotel room, and we were just getting ready, listening to music. I wasn't thinking that I was going to join him at all, but he just asked me casually whether I fancied a glass of red wine. He knew I hadn't drunk for a year, and hadn't put any pressure on me.

'Do you know what? I do,' I told him.

Liam poured me one, but didn't make a big deal out of it. As he left the room, I picked it up and took my first sip of alcohol for 12 months. At Sporting Chance, they tell you that if you drink again after rehab, you're probably dead – or at very least, would wind up back in there for another six-week programme. But I knew that I wouldn't; I had more control now, and had only used drink to compensate for other problems in my life that no longer existed. It became a habit because I wanted it to. At that moment, my brain was telling me that whatever was in that glass was not stronger than I was – it couldn't control me. Everybody is different, though, and it's a very delicate situation – for many, that kind of thought process would be very dangerous. I would hate anyone to think for a minute that I'd ever suggest it to a recovering alcoholic.

At the time, though, I didn't know why I'd been so scared to drink for such a long period, knowing deep down that I'd be able to cope with it. I went out and had a good time, perhaps having said yes in the first place because I knew that I was going out to see a girl I really liked. We'd spoken for a couple of weeks most nights before I'd even met her.

I'd got to know Leanne well on the phone but hadn't seen her in person yet. I walked over to her, for this big moment, and said, 'Hi, it's Pipes – do you want a drink babe?'

'No, I'm good thanks babe,' she said, then carried on walking up to buy her own. Wounded. *You aren't that important, mate.*

I got over Leanne fobbing me off – we've been together ever since, and I've never been happier. As it turned out,

I already knew her family really well because her brother played for Leicester in the year above me. He didn't make it in the end, but he was a brilliant player. Leanne's dad has worked for Nuneaton, scouted for Leicester, and was a very good local player when he was younger. He even knew my dad.

As anyone who has experienced blended families will know, though, there are a lot of challenges – many of which aren't always in your control. Very soon after meeting Leanne, I went away on a pre-planned holiday to Egypt with my ex, my mum and kids, just to spend some quality time with the boys. A lot of women would have done a runner there and then – but not Leanne.

A lot of my friends say she was the best thing that ever happened to me, because they saw the direction that my life was heading beforehand. After rehab, things still could have gone very wrong for me, because I was still in a vulnerable spot. You can imagine things from Leanne's perspective: before me, she was a single, hard-working mum who then suddenly had her life turned upside down by this guy who'd not long been out of rehab. He used to be a footballer, but now he was all washed up ... and he'd got three young kids. It takes a special kind of person to take that on board and make it work.

As our relationship grew, we didn't introduce Leanne to my boys until over six months down the line, when we felt ready; trying to make a new situation as comfortable as possible for them. Eventually, I moved in with her and her five-year-old daughter Sienna, but at first it was difficult: the idea of living with another man's child and not my own. I almost felt disloyal to my own kids, and it wasn't a reflection of how I felt about Sienna in any way: she is actually the most caring, easy-going and loving little girl you could hope for as a step-dad.

For a year and a half, before we moved into a bigger home, Leanne would give up her double bed to my three young boys at weekends, while we slept in the living room on a blow-up mattress. By 3am, we'd basically be grounded to the floor – but we look back on those tough moments now and smile. During times like that you truly grow together as a family.

My own life prospects were still looking a bit flat at that point, however, and filling days with new things wasn't always coming easily while I looked for the next thing in life. Slowly but surely, however, coaching began to change everything.

While working at Leicester wasn't going to give me the financial stability that I needed for the rest of my life, it had opened doors and given me a fresh focus that I needed. It was also the first in a chain of events that took me to where I am right now.

And it started with a phone call.

'We've heard you're coaching at Leicester now – can you do a kids' birthday party for me?'

By this point, my attitude had changed – I was a brand new Yes Man.

I did a couple, and the feedback from parents was beaming. There was absolutely no elite football coaching going on at those parties; it was more me thinking of what would be fun for kids. I would never claim to be a great elite coach, but I'm good with younger age groups. You turn up with a passion, lay on some different challenges and give out prizes. It felt good.

'It's my kid's birthday in three weeks – can you do that one, too?'

Yes.

I probably did four or five of these with Leanne's help. At one of the parties, a guy approached me – he was a teacher, and wondered if I did school sessions as well. I didn't – but I *could*. And that was my first proper business after becoming a footballer.

Once I put my mind to something, I go all in on it and graft. When I realised that I had this opportunity with a school, I didn't let it go. I did a taster session at Launde Primary, and it went well: the sports head offered me a couple of after-school sessions every week, and I'd get to keep the money from them. That night, I went home and wrote the letter to send out to parents. Leanne was telling me to put on it that I used to play for Leicester, but I thought it was too big-headed. So I sent it off to the teacher.

'Why haven't you put on there that you used to play for Leicester?' she said. 'I'll add it on for you.'

She was a huge City fan, and because of that, I got 32 kids for my first after-school session on a Tuesday. My good mates are grafters – bricklayers, plumbers, plasterers – who were earning £150 a day and living well back then. I was getting just under that for an hour's coaching job, something that I loved to do. Suddenly, it felt like something was coming together.

Launde offered me Thursdays, too … which sold out. Two weeks later, I drove around to 200 different schools over a week, hand-delivering letters to front offices. It's the most embarrassing thing I've ever had to do sober, I think. But off the back of those, another nine schools signed up for after-hours sessions, lunchtime football, breakfast clubs, PE cover. I was earning £1,000 per week, just doing three or four hours' coaching a day – and loving it.

There was a part of me that missed the elite side of things, though, and I felt like there was something bigger for me out there. After all, there's only so many times you can watch a kid blast a ball into an old lady's garden after you've just asked them to do a Cruyff turn.

When I was 16 or 17, I always used to wonder what happened to the lads who'd been let go from Leicester while I was getting taken on. They weren't necessarily going to get a new club – so where were they going instead?

In Sporting Chance, the seeds for owning my own academy had been sown. When I looked at someone like Jon Goodman, it made me realise that I'd love to ignite a passion in someone, and take them on to something new in their life. Through the middle part of my time in those schools, I was weighing up my options. Did I go back to somewhere like Leicester and have a proper go at things, or start something of my own that had my values attached to it?

And that's when I really started to shape the ideas behind the FSD Academy.

The first question was how I'd attach education to what I was trying to achieve. I'd have to approach schools for that, but they would need to let me have some control because there were two areas that I really wanted to bring in: life skills and football. In 2015, I approached a couple of schools but the discussions broke down about finances – I'd wanted to do something positive as a joint-venture, but it wasn't working out like that.

Understandably, schools will always consider education first in any of their thought processes. Because they were drawing the funding, they thought that they should be getting the lion's share of it for their interests. But for me, that missed the point. In many cases, kids often struggle not through education but other areas – their life situations can be completely different, and they face other challenges.

For me, a school should be somewhere to nurture young people and develop them in different ways – however that may be. Some people are suited to an academic life, but others' talents might lie elsewhere. I know I wasn't in the former category.

I approached another school, but they wanted to see something up and running before they committed. That route wasn't really working out – but then I came across a company called SCL Education, who were perfectly suited for someone like me. They had already opened 40 academies where someone with my football skill-set matched theirs, offering tutors and a full syllabus with government funding. All you had to do was find a facility to run it from.

There are a lot of academies like mine set up, where the person whose name is on it doesn't actually spend a whole lot of time there. They employ a part-time coach, a part-time teacher, and that's the extent of it. I didn't want it to be like that; I wanted to offer something more – to be there every day, making sure our life skills programme does what it should, and overseeing the day-to-day running of the academy.

One day, I went to Highfield Rangers and suggested it could be something they'd be perfect in partnering up for. They were the football club of inner-city Leicester, close to the centre, and felt like the ideal fit. Before I could even finish the sentence, they were in. At first, all we needed was the club house and football pitches; then over time, we'd build it out.

In that meeting was Owen Johnson, who sat on the board at Highfield Rangers. Owen is a great friend of Emile Heskey's, having partnered him up front in Leicester's youth teams; his son, Darnell, has also been in the club's academy since he was young and played for England's youth teams.

I'd known Owen for a long time before all of this, but had never seen him coach. When I used to clean Emile's boots I'd see him around, then later, we'd see each other out on the night scene. He also used to run a very successful clothes shop in Leicester – when I was a footballer, you either bought your gear from his place or Pilot.

Owen also had a big reputation in inner-city Leicester for developing players. He'd set up a company called Don't Just Kick It and had thoughts about the way professional academy systems were going. He was one of the first to see that although players were training regularly at their clubs, you could always invest more time as a parent to make them even better. If Owen saw a player who Darnell had come up against at under-11 level and looked better than him, he would work hard to develop him to that standard; one-on-ones down the park, working on his fitness, footwork, passing drills. Gradually, other parents on the sidelines began to realise that he'd leapt ahead of everyone else.

Off the back of that, Owen created a very successful company. People in the community who thought their kids had a bit of talent brought them to him, hoping he could take them to another level – young players who had talent, without the opportunity to work within an academy. Darnell was playing for England from a very young age, and people started to understand that Owen was doing his coaching. With his contacts, he created a powerful name for himself – if you had a talented child in the local area, you would take him to Don't Just Kick It.

After my initial meeting at Highfield Rangers, though, it turned out that it wasn't going to be such plain sailing to get things off the ground. But I didn't give up on it – and eventually, Owen and I struck up a partnership that made the FSD Academy a reality. By September 2017, we were fully up and running.

After that, it was just a case of getting kids in through the doors. Owen and I had a good skill-set between us, but in those first days I had to be honest and ask myself whether the FSD Academy at Highfield Rangers was somewhere I'd fancy sending my own kids to. The answer was a very clear no.

The place wasn't in good nick, so we had to do one of two things. Firstly, we could have just taken anyone, trying to blag it after they'd come in. Or we could try to sell them the vision of what it *would* be, not what it was then – a place with 3G pitches, a refurbished clubhouse, external classrooms, a gym, the life skills programme. Everything they couldn't see yet, I tried to sell them.

In the first year, we got 21 lads into the academy – and as I write this in 2020, we currently have 51. Two and a half years after we got things off the ground, we'd put in place all of the above – even the improved pitches, after some help from the council. I had no intention of selling parents a dream with no prospect of making things happen; it was going to, one way or another. As it turns out, I'm one of the world's best sponsorship salesmen – we've managed to raise £40,000 of additional funding to get classrooms, the gym and other equipment, all for the FSD Academy.

It's proved to be even more rewarding than I could ever have imagined. With a community feel, you get to know the kids and their lives well. I try to be an older brother rather than a dad to them – they can have fun with me, but if they step out of line then I'm going to tell them.

Every time someone new comes to the academy, I have a personal meeting with them. We sit down every few months, but the question is always the same: what is your personal target? It could be to play and enjoy football, become a mechanic or something else completely. After that we'll try to get them job placements within areas they're interested – we sent one lad to a hairdressers because he was interested in it alongside his football, and had a Saturday job there. In the end he totally changed his mind, but now he's going to university. I feel like our academy is a place to find yourself and try things.

Essentially, we try to run a mini Leicester City set-up. The lads will either have lessons or coaching in the morning and afternoon, while Wednesdays are game days, where we play other colleges. Because we've got so many students now, we have different tiers of teams. Our elite side have played Leicester and the club's Thai team so far, with other top opposition being lined up all the time. We try to give them games like that to showcase themselves in front of professional clubs, and have managed to get a few of the lads some trials.

We've tried to set up an unofficial partnership with Leicester, helping some of their boys who've had to drop out of the academy at 16. We want to be their first choice to keep them training at a good level, give them a good education and hopefully help them get back into the game.

One of the players who came to us from Leicester didn't have it easy during his time with us. When he was 17, his mum had to return to South Africa for work, leaving him and his older brother alone in Leicester to look after themselves for a while. But he was also a brilliant footballer who still had a great chance of making it in the game.

So one day, I called up one of my contacts from Sunderland and told them about him. They offered him a two-week trial immediately, but said we'd have to pay for his accommodation for a couple of weeks. So I called another former colleague up there who used to run security for the club; Tony and his wife had also housed young players during his days at the Stadium of Light, and he was still accredited to do so.

'Young lad from Leicester has got a chance at Sunderland, has he? He can stay with us.'

Leanne and I drove him up there ourselves and stayed over at Tony's, before going back home the next day. As the week went on, I was getting calls from the club telling me how well he'd been getting on there.

'He's brilliant – can't believe Leicester let him go,' one of the staff there told me.

My old club were sadly in League One at that point, so the chances of getting something looked even more promising. At the end of his trial, there was a game against Dundee that everything would rest on.

'If he plays well, we'll sign him,' they told me.

I rang my FSD lad after the game, and he told me what happened: scored two, set up two more, and Sunderland won. Brilliant. Three days later, I got another call from the club.

'Unfortunately, he didn't quite do enough – we're really sorry.'

I was gutted for him; he couldn't have done any more. But that's the harshness of trying to get a contract at a professional club when you're 17 years old. Sometimes, it doesn't matter if you're better than the other young professionals at the club – you need to be as good as those who are on the fringes of the first team. Clubs would rather stick with what they know; it didn't matter that I could vouch for my player as a great lad, because signing someone new is always a risk for them. I was so disappointed for him because he was a great kid.

In the end, he left us to join a non-league club and things are going brilliantly for him there – he's been scoring, keeping fit and generally doing really well. If he keeps it up, his opportunity with a Football League team will come eventually.

And if it doesn't? There's a whole other world out there in which he can become whatever he wants to be.

The meaning of life

MY REASONS for setting up the FSD Academy were vindicated after only a few weeks of us opening. One afternoon, I was going to buy the FSD minibus in Nottingham when my phone rang from an unknown number.

'Hi, is this Matt? It's the head security guard of the Highcross Shopping Centre. We've got one of your boys held here for shoplifting from John Lewis. He's refusing to give his parents' names – you're going to have to get here in the next hour. The police are on their way.'

My whole job at that point was looking after the welfare of these kids. I pleaded with him.

'I'm coming back now – please don't ring the police. I'll sort it.'

I bought the minibus, raced back to Leicester and headed for John Lewis. The lad was sitting there with his head bowed. He'd tried to nick some sweets.

'Let me take him,' I said to the guard. 'He knows he's done wrong. You have my word that his mum or dad will come back in with him and sort this out.'

Eventually, after about 15 minutes, he relented. I felt like a chat-shit champion – my mum would have been proud. When we got out, the kid was buzzing.

'I've never seen anyone get out of a situation like that! You are the best! I'm so pleased my mum and dad aren't going to find out.'

Er … no. I laid it out to him.

'There's no way you're shoplifting at my academy and your mum and dad aren't finding out about it. It's just better they hear it from me, my way, than theirs.'

He was terrified, but I drove him home, reintroduced myself to his mum and told her. He'd been brilliant for me up to that point, but had let himself down that day. Nothing would come of it, but from this point he needed to learn some lessons. Afterwards, he told me that it was the first time he'd done something like that and hadn't been beaten at home for it.

Owen and I both deal with incidents like this, but we count it as part of our life-skills programme. That kid now plays for Leicestershire's futsal team, has been on a trial at Shepshed Dynamo, has a full-time job in care work where he looks after vulnerable people overnight, has passed his Level 2 and 3 coaching badges, plus a personal training gym qualification. And the best part? FSD have now offered him their first ever full-time coaching position. From shoplifting in his first five weeks, to this. That's why we do this.

I'm very lucky that I have my academy, but even luckier to have my family. Leanne and I are so lucky that everyone gets on as well as they do in our house together, but that didn't just happen by chance. She is the glue that holds our family together, and the single-biggest influence in shaping my life after rehab. I know it's corny to talk about soulmates, but I'd never experienced anything like that before meeting her; the kind of person who strikes a great balance between keeping me in check and showing love for her family.

The best thing you can wish for your own children is that they're happy, and that's my sole purpose in life today. As I write this, the four kids are all playing *Fortnite* together in their rooms; sometimes, I'll just stand outside their bedroom doors listening to them laughing away with each other.

I sometimes worry that I spend too much time with the youngsters at my academy, but I want to show my boys what kind of person I am and try to set the best example I can for them now. Every dad wants their kids to look at them and feel proud – and that's what gets me up every day. I want to be that person who people can look at and feel trust in, whether it's a mate in a tight spot who needs a hand, or one of my own kids who's missed their bus and needs a lift home.

My eldest lad, Brandan, is a born Mackem – a Sunderland native, if you weren't sure – and reminds me so much of myself when I was his age: quiet, unassuming, polite and an all-round kind soul. He's got so much potential in life. Finlay is my fearless, wild and very loving middle son – and a huge Leicester fan who goes to the King Power Stadium every week with his grandad. When he puts his heart into something, he puts everything in, and that always makes me so proud to see.

My youngest boy, Kairo, is in Burton Albion's academy system right now – I've told him many times that he is a lot more talented than me at his age. As the littlest of our four kids, he's got the most fight within him. He's at least three years younger than any of them, so has that extra determination about him even when he's playing in the garden.

But I try to be as laid back with him about his football as possible. Other parents sometimes ask me why I don't shout at him when he's playing, and I'm sure a few of them think I don't care about whether he makes it or not. But it's nothing like that: he just doesn't need any pressure coming from me. My dad once asked me whether I was gutted that Kai doesn't look at me while he's playing. But he's not supposed to, is he? He listens to his coach, looks where the ball is, and where his team-mates are. If he's looking at me, there's a problem. Every now and again at half-time, he'll have a little glance up at me because I'm his dad. If he's shocking – and sometimes he is – then he'll get a little thumbs up. In the car we'll have a little chat about the game, but that's it. He doesn't need all of those different voices in his head like I had.

Since I came out of Sporting Chance, my life has been geared towards positivity and taking myself out of the comfort zone. In 2014, I set up MPTV on YouTube with a few football coaching videos, trying to do something different in an area where I was far from confident. Ultimately, though, those fumbling videos led to something good: my return to the airwaves on BBC Radio Leicester. As you know by now, the first spell involved me being steaming or stripped of mental capacity on Valium – but I also never prepared at all. I was just trying to wing it from an ex-footballer's point of view, which was never going to work: not least when I could barely string a sentence together.

On the bright side, improving the second time around was always going to be a low bar to clear. If you look back at the first MPTV videos now, they're shocking – I'm spilling words all over the place, coming across as shy and uncomfortable. But the more you practise, the more you increase in confidence and develop your own style.

Matt Elliott's time on Radio Leicester was coming to an end as the ex-player summariser in early 2017, and that meant there was a vacancy to fill. Ian Stringer had been the main commentator when I was bumbling around like a joker alongside him, but I've got so much time for him – the fact that he reached out and gave me another chance meant a lot. He left me a voicemail boosting me up, saying he'd seen my MPTV work, and wondered if I could cover a weekend game with him. To give me another opportunity when I'd let him down before was a big thing.

The old me might have said no – but not Yes Man. So I accepted. At first, I was picking up the odd game as cover for Matty when he was doing other work, but I used to get incredibly nervous before going on air. In the end, Radio Leicester gave me the permanent gig in 2018/19, but it was six months and a lot of games before I genuinely felt comfortable doing it. I'm not going to claim that I'm the world's greatest summariser these days, but from where I started to where I am now is a long way.

I'd always hated being on TV, too – but when the BBC asked me to front an *Inside Out* documentary about racism in grassroots football in 2020, I said yes again. I was bricking it: there was no script … nothing. Afterwards, though, I got some lovely phone calls once the show had aired; it hadn't been anywhere near as bad as I had thought.

When it comes to my football career, I don't feel protective about keeping it a big, fluffy dream. Maybe it's because I never got that legacy of 500 league appearances, cup wins, Champions League experience or anything like that. Some of the ex-footballers I've spoken to think I'm crazy with some of the things I tell in public now, but then I ask myself: *why?* It's just the truth – it's my story.

I've got nothing to hide, but so much to feel blessed for in life today: an amazing wife, four incredible children between us and everything to look forward to in the years ahead. I wasn't happy being a Premiership footballer. I wasn't happy earning £10,000 per week. I wasn't happy when freedom from it all finally came.

I used to live for nights out after all of that, trying to compensate for the loss of my football career. Now, nothing gives me more pleasure than being at Bradgate Park with the family, taking our dog Sonny for a walk, and getting coffee and bacon sandwiches at the café.

This is happiness.

Acknowledgements

WHEN YOU write your life story and go back through everything, you realise just how fortunate you are to have so many amazing people in your life. It's at this point that I'd like to acknowledge some of them, because they deserve it. Their support, however big or small, has helped shape who I am today.

First of all, my mum's love and unwavering support throughout both highs and lows pulled me through and gave me the strongest foundations to build on, moving forward. She is a very special person, and I love her with everything I have.

Dad: we've had our ups and downs, but throughout everything I've always had that comfortable feeling of knowing you're there to back me up no matter what. Your support for myself, Leanne and the kids is appreciated every day. Much love, Pops.

My brother, Dan: we were inseparable as kids and remain best mates as adults. A better sibling would be impossible to wish for – thanks for everything, Broski. Also, a huge thanks to my lovely sister-in-law Laura and beautiful niece Luna for making Dan so happy. I love you all. Thanks also to my older brother, Keith.

Thank you to my soulmate, Leanne. Over time we've learned that great relationships don't just happen: they take time, patience, effort and two people who truly want to be together. We haven't got everything, but we've got all we need in our beautiful kids and each other. Love you, baby.

To Brandan, Sienna, Finlay and Kairo: you make me strive to be a better man, dad and step-dad every day. I love you with all my heart.

I would also like to thank Leanne's incredibly supportive family, who accepted me with open arms and have always shown me plenty of love. You all contribute to our lives so much.

Not only am I fortunate to have the love and support of family, but I also have an incredible network of friends and work colleagues. Some are mentioned directly in this book, others aren't, but their support, advice, friendship and guidance means so much to me. You'll know who you are, and I love and appreciate every single one of you.

Carl Heggs has been great for me. I'm a bit of a soft touch, but he's been good at helping me to assert myself more over the years. Nick Oakley, meanwhile, comes from a completely different background to me but is one of my most trusted confidants. I often lean on him for advice, and I think a lot of my positivity has come from chats with him.

Matt Depaepe has *always* been there for me. He was the guy I'd try to make come out with me the most, and sometimes he would – not drinking, just to make sure I wouldn't get myself into trouble. He stayed with me through it all, good times and bad.

Nick Hutchins was someone who I always felt like I could talk to after I came out of rehab, just being honest and open about everything. When I felt like I didn't need the support of counselling and AA meetings so much, he was the guy I could always discuss my life with – and at times, I think I was helping him as much as he was helping me. That ability to be open and honest with someone you trust is a powerful thing.

James Miller has been one of my best friends for over two decades and will be for the rest of my life. Thank you for all the memories, brother – and there are still plenty more to create.

I met Rob O'Donnell quite some time after leaving rehab, but he very quickly became one of my closest friends. He is a very successful person but so down to earth, and I could tell from the outset that he genuinely wanted the best for me and my family. Our wives Tracey and Leanne are very close, and all of our kids love Rob and Tracey's son, Archie. Robbo is a top man with a beautiful family.

ACKNOWLEDGEMENTS

Thanks to those at BBC Radio Leicester, too: particularly Ian Stringer, Owynn Palmer-Atkin, Dale Neal, Jason Bourne and Ady Dayman, who have all been brilliant with their friendship and support on the airwaves.

Liam Deacy has become a good friend and was the one who pushed me to do this book in the first place.

A huge thanks to the writer of it, Joe Brewin, whose patience, support and guidance throughout this process has been outstanding. I would also like to thank Pitch Publishing for giving me the platform to tell my story, and their talented designer, Duncan Olner.

Thank you to everyone at Sporting Chance: James, Tony, Julian, Chris and Peter, God rest his soul – and not forgetting my compadres, John, Ryan and Ray.

In the wider football community, Brian Deane has always been there for me; Muzzy Izzet gave me so much of his time when I was setting up the FSD Academy, while my old Leicester City colleagues Jon Stevenson, Matt Heath, Micky Adams, Garry Parker, Dave Rennie, Matt Elliott, Gerry Taggart, Steve Walsh, Stefan Oakes, Jordan Stewart, Frank Sinclair, Robert Purdie, Guy Branston and Julian Joachim have all been really supportive and great friends over the years. From Sunderland, exactly the same sentiments go to Pete Friar and Kevin Ball. Special mentions to Debbie, Gina and Louise from Leicester: thank you for everything, ladies.

I also can't forget the former club reverend, Bruce Nadin, who supported me through some desperate times of despair – and big thanks also to Paul Cheney, Mark Jackson, Chris Tucker, Steve Beaglehole, Paul McAndrew, Rob Owen, Harj Hir, Alan Birchenall, Dr Ian Patchett, Dale Bradshaw and Jon Rudkin.

I also thank Verity, as the time we shared together produced our three beautiful sons. I'm also so appreciative to Jenny, 'Gray' and Dave for being superb grandparents.

People come into our lives at different times and for different reasons, but I'm very glad these guys came into mine. Thank you and much love to: Ian Anderson, Matty Williams, Dean Halford, Ryan and Ash Kilby, Ryan Ryiatt, Mark Rossiter, Chris Putnam, Jake Morris, Jonny Langmaid, Gary Jones, Owen and Erica Johnson, all of our students at the FSD Academy, Carl Talents, Ian Bannister, Ainsley Neckles, Toby and Carl Fura, Rish, Rav and Avi from Hillmoren, Chris Whittingham and Sam Hagger from the Beautiful Pubs Collective, Vix, Jocelyn Johnson, Steve Booth, Alex Mortimer, Soloman Paul, Sam Morton, Jimmy Shemi, Craig Heggs, Steve Plews, Simon Crabtree, Paul Culpin, Lee Harriman, Tom Meighan, Darren Fletcher, Dean and Kyle Wright, Andrew Wilson, Simon and Mandy Flude, Darren Webb, Gogs, Steve Orme, Kirk Master, Jersey and Kayleigh Budd, Jo Hextall, Matt Baker, Lee Marlow, Mick McCarthy, Mike McCarthy, Mac and Mike at the Black Horse, Andrew

Mills, Matt Nurse, Ryan Sutherington, Marc Shultz, Bob Thomas, Patricia and Charlotte Leeds, Jeff Peters, Priti Coles, Chef Shaf at Chutney Ivy, Rich and Dave Clay, the Aston family, Rob Tanner, Leanne Poole, Clint, Sarah and Martin at Highfield Rangers, Gerry Burke, Tango, Tony Thorpe, Tony Burridge, Trev Benjamin, Ade Akinbiyi, Alison Tripney, Andy Palmer, Bill Wall, Brian Anderson, Leroy Moore, Darryl Burgess, Dave and the team at Koi Sports, David and Natalie Bell, David Garcia, Dev Kumar Parmar, Gareth Mordey, Jemma George, Ross Brittleton, John Hutchinson, Namrata Varia, Uncle Frank Benbini, Summaya Mughal, Adam Whitty, Jimmy Carpenter, Liam Gibbs, Kamlesh Purohit, Mark and Sophie Shardlow, Nick Hodges at the Bodie Hodges Foundation, Pascal Chimbonda, Paul McCue, Karl Simmons, Ashley Chambers, Wes Blocko and Roy Cole.

If I've missed anyone, I'm so sorry. Thank you all so much for being part of my journey.

Pipes x

Also available at all good book stores

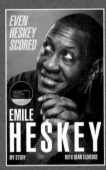

9781785315008

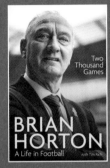

9781785316685

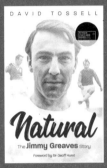

9781785314902

9781785314995

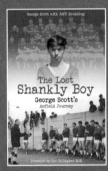

9781785316784

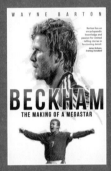

9781785316760

9781785315510

9781785316333

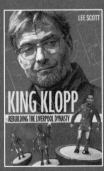

9781785316500